Look Back 75

Ted Sharpe

Printed and bound in England by www.printondemand-worldwide.com

http://www.fast-print.net/bookshop

Look Back 75

Text and illustrations copyright © Ted Sharpe 2017

A catalogue record for this book is available from the British Library

ISBN 978-178456-490-2

First published 2017 by
FASTPRINT PUBLISHING
Peterborough, England.

Foreword

B ecause of the war the Forties played a pivotal role in shaping the second half of the twentieth century. Those years witnessed change on a hitherto unimaginable scale and nowhere was that more evident than in the countryside. Living through those years though it can truthfully be said, that thanks to our inbred human capacity to adapt to change, we were quite, quite unaware of the magnitude of what was taking place before us.

My own stamping ground centred on a large sporting estate in the glorious county of Shropshire, where my father was head-gamekeeper and my grandfather was bailiff, or in modern parlance, farm manager of its home farm. Looking back now though what an unbelievable difference there is between the world of my youth and that which we live in today.

My original motivation for these writings was to create for my grandchildren a picture of the countryside in which my generation grew up. On sober reflection though it has to be doubted whether they, poor souls reared in this cosseted era of Hi-tech and square screens, could even begin to imagine, let alone connect, with those long gone days.

Undaunted though, and blessed with a streak of natural stubbornness, I have persisted. Inevitably these writings recall that world of considerable happiness in which we grew up; helped now and again of course by a snippet garnered in more recent years.

Contents

1. Nothing But The Night

It was during that terrible war of 1914-18 and on the day in question Grandfather Davis had returned home extremely disturbed. Perhaps distressed would be a better word for he had met a friend, their neighbour as it happened, who farmed adjoining land. As they had chatted across the boundary hedge Grandfather had begun to sense unease, a certain agitation, which was completely out of character.

At first they had discussed things in general; things like food shortages and the ever-increasing problem of losing good horses to the requisition agents who were scouring the countryside. It was not only young men who were needed for fuelling the war. Many a farmer drove a valuable nag to market only to return home on foot!

As invariably happened when they met, conversation drifted to the lads at the front. Grandfather had a younger brother serving with the Shropshire Yeomanry whilst his neighbour had three sons over there. Only a day or so earlier one of them, Jack by name, had written to say he was expecting to get leave shortly and from that moment preparations for his home-coming had been top priority. You may guess the effort which was being put in to make his stay enjoyable. There would have to be a day or two ferreting, a favourite occupation, a bit of horse riding, visits to friends, relatives, old haunts, anything in fact to take his mind off what he had left behind! Neighbours too had joined in by raiding their larders to help his mother ensure the inner man would be well and truly catered for.

Naturally Grandfather enquired whether there was any more news of Jack yet. Instead of giving a direct answer his friend recounted the events of the previous night. As his story unfolded the reason for his agitation became increasingly and painfully clear. Determined not to be caught out by their son arriving home early, his wife had worked late on a final batch of cooking. He had stayed up to keep her company and to help out where he could. By the time they finally went to bed the midnight hour had long since struck. After they had been in bed a while he was awakened by his wife. "Listen! I can hear a pony and trap". He listened but could hear nothing. But she persisted. "There it is again. It's louder now". This time he too could hear it, louder then gone again, as noise does at night when bends in the road or dense patches of hedge or thicket, not to mention the vagaries of wind, all contrive to play tricks with sound.

Now there could be no doubting it was a pony and trap rattling along. "It's our Jack! said his wife "he's home earlier than he thought. He's managed to find a carrier in Wellington to drive him out". Her husband urged caution. It could be anyone, the doctor, the vet or just a neighbour out late. They would only know for certain if it turned off the road.

They lay still and listened. Sure enough there came the break in rhythm and change of sound as it turned into their farm drive. You can imagine the rush to dash downstairs and light a lamp in the hallway. All the time they could hear the trap rattling closer. They heard the "Whoa" from the driver and the rattling stopped to be replaced by scrape of hoof and creak of harness. Bolts were yanked back and the door flung open as they fairly flew outside to welcome their son.

But where was he? Where was Jack? Where was the pony; and the trap; and the carrier? Where indeed? For nothing was there! Nothing - but the night.

"We must have been mistaken Mother. It must have carried on along the road". It was not so much a statement as a prayer. But his prayer went unanswered. In vain they listened. Of pony and trap not a sound. Just the chewing of cud in the stockyard, the plaintive cry of a peewit across the fields, scrape of hoof in the stable, shrill of moorhen from a nearby pond. Utterly bewildered, thoroughly shaken and no doubt very frightened, they returned inside, bolted the door and went back to bed. It is a sure fact they were not going to sleep – but what else could they do?

That then is the story my grandfather brought home and related in the kitchen of the old farmhouse at Charlton Hill. He was terribly upset

for he knew, as did my mother and grandmother who listened to him, as indeed their poor friends must have known only too well, that Jack would not be coming home.

A day or so later they learned Jack had indeed died on the night of the pony. He had taken part in a raid across no-mans-land, a highly perilous occupation at the best of times. And so it had proved. "And can you really be so simple as to believe a tale like that"? I hear my grandchildren ask, their voices charged with disbelief and incredulity. Products of this objective, scientific, pragmatic materialistic age what else would you expect the poor things to say? But you see I knew the people involved. More honest, reliable, down to earth folk you will never come across. Oh yes! I believe it alright ---- every single word!

2. Never Close The Window

"Early to bed and early to rise, maketh man healthy, wealthy and wise."

Or so one or other of my grandmothers invariably and infuriatingly intoned as I was despatched up the stairs. Protests that it was far too early for bed went unheeded by my late beloved mother. Everyone it seemed knew exactly what was best for the boy Edward. Sadly in my case that gem has proved spectacularly incorrect on both counts! Fortunately they were all of the same mind concerning bedroom windows. No matter what the weather they had to be open and through them carried the sounds of the outside world so cruelly denied.

Sometimes there was nothing to hear but the wind as it buffeted the house and swished through treetops. At other times a downpour drowned all other noise as it drummed on tiles and cascaded into guttering. But as the downpour eased to drizzle and the cascade a mere trickle, or as the gale faded to a breeze one gradually became aware of a host of other sounds. Noises which had remained hidden were suddenly emerging as do trees with the lifting of a mist.

On a really still evening the snarl of fallow bucks rutting, occasionally even the rattle of antlers as they met in combat. Bats squeaked as they hawked their prey into summer darkness. Loud quacking of wild-duck acorning around the edges of Long Pool shattered many a wintery night and occasionally during really hard weather, the whistle of widgeon. Blackbird's song or bedtime chant was often heard and nightjar's incessant churring. Occasionally a pause, then off he went again his monotonous buzz rising and falling with variation in the waft of a slight breeze.

A muffled rattle of chain through ring as the horse stabled below reached up for hay, sometimes a snort or stamp of hoof. Those were friendly sounds by any standards. Eyrie cry from waterhen flighting high in the night sky, thrush singing from telegraph wires, hoots and whistles from Severn Valley steam locos followed by the puff and rattle of their progress, sometimes quite loud then suddenly gone as they passed through numerous cuttings and breaks of dense timber.

Moorhen and coot, territorial and aggressive calling from the pool, mistle thrush, equally aggressive challenging from the topmost branch of an ash tree and from a blackthorn thicket along the edge of Spring Coppice, that rusty brown maestro now singing to the stars, the nightingale.

A cow calling long and plaintively, bawling for her newly weaned calf. Sometimes an answering blart from the object of her dismay. A chaffinch pink-pinking, constant cawing and chatter of rooks loudly protecting and feeding nests of young. French partridge calling incessantly, most probably perched on top of a gate, chick-chic-a-dee, chick-chick-a-dee, neck puffing and swelling in monotonous indignation. Wren churring angrily and scurry and squeak of mice in the ceiling.

Shriek of little owls. Hunting horns, winded at intervals through the night as keepers kept foxes away from young pheasants newly moved to woods. Urgent crying of grey partridges newly flown to jug in open fields. Chizzz-uck, Chizzz-uck, as they gathered and encircled for yet another watchful night. Hum of Severn Valley diesel cars and melodious two-tone horn. Sheep blarting, ewes yelling for lambs, lambs yelling for ewes, newly encamped around the Sheepcots ready for shearing.

Chatter of jackdaws, shriek and hoot of owls. Urgent beating of swan wings as they took off from Long Pool followed by the regular steady whistle of mighty wingbeats as they headed for Severn. Church clock striking, sonorous and mellow, stark contrast to the raucous incessant cries of young tawny owls demanding food, each from his own treetop.

Bark of dog fox thrice repeated, cry of nesting plover, master of flashing wingbeat, roosters waking to bright moonlight and crowing manfully to the world in general. One could almost hear their drowsy spouses muttering to the old fool to get back under his wing! On a really still night the lighter urgent chimes of the school clock, always that little bit behind St Chads, always hurrying to catch up.

Screech of vixen, eyrie and unearthly. Cry of curlew, melodious and haunting, flying high on passage to the Welsh Marches. Cuckoos frequently, and very occasionally wild-geese. Hounds of the sky, wild indeed and mysterious, flighting no doubt between estuaries of Severn and Dee. Buzz and rattle of car wheels on park grid gates. Twitter of swallows, grating of corncrake, purr of turtledove and shriek of swift. Frank of heron, as their cry was known, and invariably on a spring evening the sound of a roading woodcock. Churr-churr-churr-croak repeated at regular short intervals as he patrolled his aerial boundary into the gloaming. Lie still and listen for a few minutes and round he came again accurate it seemed to the yard and the second. Wood pigeon wing-clapping, cry of cock pheasant and whirr of wings.

Cry of cock pheasant. For me that recalls the sound which transcended all others. Pheasants in a great stretch of woodland known as The Terrace. Often a car backfiring or blast from open cast coal mining disturbed them at night. Startled into sudden wakefulness every single cock called out from his roost. Then a fantastic, nerve tingling wave of sound welled up in Stockton End to sweep along that great length of woodland finally rippling and fading away down the valley of Severn. Like the voices of some ghostly massed choir it never failed to thrill.

3. Wartime Recollections 1939-1945

During the Thirties a new cinema was built in Bridgnorth. It was called the Majestic and that is where, at the tender age of four, I was taken to see my first film. Apart from a fellow waving a bit of paper as he climbed down the steps from an aeroplane, and then speaking through microphones to the crowd waiting to greet him, I recall very little of it.

What I can recall is my mother on one side of me explaining that thanks to Mr Chamberlain there would not now be a war. At the same time my father on the other side was fuming that war was now a certainty. Well do I recall Mother's futile attempts to hush him up because his very audible remarks were not being well received. No way was this warmonger going to be allowed to shatter the dream of that cinema audience, the dream that desperate and unhappy Prime Minister had conjured up for them –the dream of peace in their time!

Anyway what was this thing being spoken about, this thing called war. Clearly from the reactions of the grownups it was something very unpleasant, and despite their determination to carry on as normal, the sense of foreboding and fear was inescapable.

In 1939 we went on a short motoring holiday to Scotland. I can clearly recall visiting Stirling Castle and Father talking to a Sergeant Black with whom he had served in World War I: also the bawling and shouting as squads of recruits were being drilled. On the journey up we had crossed the Firth of Forth by the ferry and had a wonderful view of battleships of the North Sea fleet at anchor there. All very exciting for a small boy.

Funnily enough I have no recollections of the actual outbreak of war. Doubtless the atmosphere engendered at home by Father's blunt refusal to ignore stark reality reduced this cataclysmic event to a mere formality. All around though things were happening swiftly and I enjoyed the great asset of parents who kept me fully informed wherever they deemed it suitable. Church bells would no longer be rung: they were to be used only as the warning of invasion. Invasion? What was an invasion? Gas attacks on the other hand were to be notified by wardens wielding wooden rattles. Marvellous devices comprising a cogwheel and striking board which produced a racket akin to a machine gun. Gas masks were issued to everyone, even babies, and for the first year or two of the war we carried them with us at all times. Fear of gas really did grip the population. Its use in World War I had left bitter memories, and with the new realism which had replaced the earlier reluctance to face facts, few doubted Hitler would hesitate to use it. Hitler! That was the name on everybody's lips.

Air raids too became something of a national phobia long before they actually occurred. Of course the grown-ups had seen what had happened in Spain. Windows in all public buildings and most town houses were criss-crossed with brown sticky paper to help prevent flying glass in the event of bombing. Doorways of public buildings, police and fire stations, schools etc. were protected from blast, at least in theory, by walls of sandbags. Air raid shelters, named after a chap called Anderson, appeared in the gardens of countless town houses and for those without a shelter the drill was to sleep under the kitchen table or in the cupboard beneath the stairs! Communal shelters were built in the playgrounds of many of the town schools.

Then of course there was the Blackout. Town centres became pitch black on a dark night. Street lights had been extinguished for the duration. Blackout curtains covered every window. Car headlights were fitted with covers which allowed an aperture the size of an old penny piece, about an inch and a quarter I would guess –anyway enough to prevent speeding! Even railway engines were fitted with black tarpaulins, hung from the back of the open cab roof and over the coal tender so the glow from the firebox could not be spotted from the air. The air raid warden's cry of "Put that light out!" became a national catch phrase. People groped their way about blackened streets, torch in hand, but not daring to use it for fear of annoying the warden. Worse still they might run down the batteries which by now were becoming akin to gold dust. Never fear though, in order that worthy citizens should not collide in the darkness, some crackpot in a ministry combined science with patriotic fervour to produce millions of little pin-on badges. They were shaped "V" (for victory) and painted with luminous paint. Doubtless he duly appeared in the honours lists!

Hitler had already used incendiary bombs during his Blitzkreig in Europe and it was assumed, quite correctly, they would soon shower down on British towns and cities. I do not remember the criteria for ownership but in no time at all just about everyone seemed to be the proud possessor of a stirrup-pump. A demonstration on their use was laid on in the village. It was held on the road just outside Joe Peake's smithy and was conducted by a fellow from the local Fire Brigade, ably supported by P.C.Layton, who also doubled up as Master of Ceremonies.

First they got a nice little fire started with rags and petrol, then extinguished it with buckets of sand. A repeat performance with buckets of water and then finally the piece de resistance, the stirrup pump! The pump itself was a vertical cylinder with a pumping handle at one end and with a length of hosepipe leading to a nozzle attached to the side of it. The cylinder was stood in a bucket of water and held upright by a parallel metal bar with an out –turned foot on which was placed a human foot. Get the idea? Well never mind! A hefty volunteer was found to do the pumping and despite the best efforts of him, the fireman, and the constable, the fire continued to flourish and finally had to be extinguished by more conventional means.

Everyone went home happy that incendiary bombs would be a minor irritant and red painted buckets filled with sand appeared in all manner of places. Happily most never saw active service except as convenient receptacles for cigarette ends. Shortly after this the public were warned to keep away from incendiaries for at least five minutes after ignition. Hitler, it appeared, had perfected one with a delayed explosive device. That I believe was my first real lesson in man's apparently limitless ingenuity in contriving new weapons of destruction. I rather suspect such a device may have caused the fatal injury to Grannie Sue's uncle Dick Ward when trying to extinguish a fire in a Belfast hospital.

Air power was clearly going to be a major factor in this war. During the early days I well recall being taken over to Cosford aerodrome to see the Harvard trainers which were being imported from America.

They were snub nosed and noisy and their characteristic whine soon became the background to everyday life as the rush to train pilots really got under way.

It would be foolish to pretend our age group were really aware of what was happening in the overall conduct of the war. We became aware for example that Hitler, for we tended to think of Germany as Hitler, had conquered the rest of Europe. We did realise that a fleet of small ships had pulled off a miraculous rescue of most of our own and some of the French army, (some 338,000 I recently learned). We could hardly not have known for the government turned it into a major propaganda coup. Listening to the grown-ups you would think we had achieved a major victory! People simply refused to accept reality.

In recent years there have been numerous reports that morale in the civilian population was low and the majority, given the option, would have sued for peace. All I can say is that every adult with whom I had any contact, or who had any influence on my upbringing, conveyed but two facts. One. Hitler was evil and had to be beaten. Two. Hitler would be beaten!

But going back to Dunkirk. That I think was when my age group really began to grasp, not the horror, but the general idea of what was happening around us. We learned very quickly though, and by the end of hostilities some five years down the line were seasoned observers.

Suddenly we knew there really was a war on. Most of the fellows eligible for call-up had already joined the services. When they returned home on leave their uniforms added to the general atmosphere, but as time went on, and they were posted to various theatres of war, these visits became few and far between. Some fellow pupils at school waved goodbye to their fathers for the duration.

On the Home Front rationing became the major concern. There were ration books for food, coupons for clothing, and coupons for petrol. Sweets and chocolate were rationed and imported fruits disappeared. Coal was rationed and doubtless many other items I forget. Apart from all these things officially rationed just about anything you might care to mention became difficult. Film for cameras was unobtainable, torch batteries like gold dust, and towards the end of their working life people used to warm them in the oven to extract the last few lumens! Old codgers who had refused to forsake their carbide cycle lamps were satisfyingly vindicated. Carbide was also great stuff for popping in ink wells at school, the resultant mess of black foam spewing across the desk lid of the form swot quite spectacular.

New bicycles were rare and new cars nonexistent. At school writing paper and exercise books contained a large proportion of straw and pencils were unpainted. All consumer goods had to carry an official stamp. I never really knew the reason for that but it was known as the "Utility Mark".

What was known as the War Effort built up at an amazing rate and it affected everyone and every aspect of life. For instance all the sign posts were removed. This, or so it was said, was to hinder the movement of spies, fifth columnists or invading German troops! It certainly hindered the British army on its seemingly endless manoeuvres. Progress of vehicles usually consisted of dashes from a map reading session at one cross-roads to more map reading at the next cross-roads. Good map reading practice no doubt and anyway there was usually a fair presence of locals to help out, or even hinder if addressed in the wrong manner!

Army engineers created a simulated river crossing in Apley Park. A rope was stretched between two trees approximately 20 ft. above the placid waters of the Black Pool. Troops shinned up a tree on this side with the help of a rope, crossed in the approved manner and descended by rope on the far side. A steel punt paddled around below to rescue any who failed to make it. None did which was disappointing for us lads.

On another occasion the little brook running through the park was dammed to create a pond for motor cycle despatch riders to negotiate. From the local youngsters point of view this was far more rewarding as the odd one did come unstuck.

Military camps were springing up all over the place. The R.A.F. established a large training establishment at Stanmore outside Bridgnorth and odd little groups of Nissen huts, usually built in woodland, dotted the countryside.

Brick and concrete pillboxes sprouted like mushrooms at all sorts of strategic points such as crossroads and bridges. In the event of invasion they were to be manned by local Home Guard units. One highly conspicuous specimen overlooked the suspension bridge crossing the Severn at Linley.

It so happened that on a tour of inspection of the area the G.O.C. Western Command asked Father, then in command of the local platoon, how many men he proposed to deploy in it. To the horror of the attendant brass Father said " I wouldn't put a rabbit in the damn thing – let alone a man. It's simply a death trap!"

"So what would you propose instead?" asked the General somewhat taken aback.

"A series of slit trenches with a concealed approach and a wide field of fire". At the time they were standing on the edge of dense woodland overlooking the bridge and its approaches.

"Well I suggest you do that", said the General clearly impressed by the idea.

"You are standing on the edge of one", said Pa. He was too! Time as a sniper during W War 1 had not been wasted! True to form the General then set about lecturing his entourage that this was what he wanted to see in future! It's a strange old world.

Apart from the forces there was enormous activity on the Civilian front. In addition to the A.R.P. and Home Guard there was the Royal Observer Corps, whilst the Police having lost so many men of military age relied heavily on the Special Constabulary. Also of course countless men and women were recruited for work in the munitions factories.

Gamekeepers and gardeners past call-up age moved onto the farms which had again been hit by loss of the younger men. Young ladies in Land Army attire appeared on the farms, many of them city girls. What a change it must have been for them and what a marvellous contribution they made to the Nation's food supply.

Talking of food supply brings to mind the great slogan "Dig for Victory". From the onset of hostilities everyone was aware of the risk of starvation. Things had been pretty sticky following the U-Boat campaign in World War I. They could be a damn sight worse this time round. So dig they did. Lawns and flower beds were dug up for vegetable growing in people's gardens. On the farms horn gave way to corn and sports fields and parkland came under the plough. In October the senior schools in rural areas all gave their pupils a fortnight's potato picking "holiday".

Everybody was encouraged to feed their household waste to chickens or a pig and households which registered to do so received coupons to purchase what was optimistically called "Balancer Meal". "Dig for Victory" could be hailed as a brilliant propaganda success. In actual fact the population knew the score only too well and needed little encouragement to supplement those meagre rations. Well I recall my grandmother who lived alone in Bridgnorth once showing me her rations for the week. Churchill, or so the story went, had asked to be shown the ration allowance for an individual. On being shown he commented that he could manage very nicely on it for a day. "But the problem is Sir", the official said, "that is for a week!" Suffices to say – they were pretty meagre. Manual workers did in fact receive an extra supplement but be assured they would not have got fat on it.

But of course Grannie did not live on her rations. She ran a good little veg garden and we kept her supplied with many extras. Fruit, honey, occasionally butter, an odd rabbit or chicken or eggs. This was true of most town people the majority of whom had friends or relatives in the country. Then of course there was the Black Market based mainly on meat and eggs. Pigs and poultry contributed most of the meat and many farmers plied the trade to a greater or lesser degree. It was of course a high risk occupation. Farmers did nicely out of it, but- and I stress this, most played the game and sold at a price which Joe Public could afford. Bear in mind there was full employment and wages in the towns were at an all time high. Having said all that, a great many of the really poor in the inner cities must have been very, very hungry; they also, poor beggars, bore the brunt of the bombing which was to follow. Meat and sugar were probably the two items where rationing hit hardest and a host of magic recipes claiming to replace the need for such essentials appeared in every paper and magazine. All kinds of amazing cakes and pies were concocted. I recall Mother making a sponge cake with liquid paraffin instead of margarine. It ate and tasted extremely well, its only drawback being that L.P. still did its deadly work. So that was short lived. The only other experiments I can remember were various pies and marmalades involving carrots whilst potatoes became a wonder food!

In Norton the W.I. became the local centre for a massive nationwide knitting campaign.. Balaclavas and scarves in khaki, sea-boots, stock- ings, and sweaters in greased wool. Kids at school were roped into this network. I knitted away at a khaki scarf which grew but slowly and ever narrower as stitches were dropped. Lessons in First Aid were a priority for most Ladies organisations. Norton W.I. decided to train in the use of firearms and Father was asked to instruct them. Despite his best efforts it was decided after the initial session that it might be better if they stuck to First Aid!

Preserving of home-grown fruit and tomatoes became the in thing. Bottling and indeed canning groups, again mainly through the W.I., were set up in most villages and ran for years.

There were waste paper collection rounds. These were organised by local ladies and manned by schoolkids on Saturday mornings. They ran for a year or two and then fizzled out: not I hasten to say through lack of commitment, but simply because the supply of paper dried up. Newspapers had been rapidly reduced to four pages i.e. one double sheet. Carrier bags were a thing of the past and items such as bread loaves and fruit, anything which would not otherwise fall apart, were simply not wrapped. With boots to dry, fires to light and lavatory paper in short supply you can understand why the collection job fizzled out. A similar scheme was launched for rags, but again with clothes rationing anything lucky or tough enough to become a rag usually ended up as cleaning material; or as part of the ubiquitous rag-mat since carpets and coconut door-mats were but a memory from yesteryear. Knitting wools too were unobtainable and our mothers made new garments out of old ones by first unravelling and then re-knitting the wool.

Early in the war scrap metal became a top priority. People with iron railings or gates round the front of their gardens were apt to find them being cut off and loaded onto a lorry. If you look around many older properties in towns, you can still see the rows of iron stubs where low walls were once topped with railings. It was said locally that the famous Iron Bridge only survived because of the difficulties involved in demolishing it!

Apart from petrol rationing great efforts were made to use alternative energy sources. Woodland was being felled all over the country and with coal rationed, the tops were sawn into logs. A great many lorries and buses ran on petrol rather than diesel at that time. It was found they could be fuelled by gas and quite a number were converted. Instead of filling up with petrol they pulled a trailer with a tank of gas behind; not unlike overgrown 45 gallon drums as I remember them. Those old steam lorries, mainly Sentinels and Fodens, which had been on the verge of extinction, found an unexpected ally in the German U-Boat and carried on working well into the war.

One day Father returned home with lengths of silk parachute cord attached to torn rubber sheeting. It was part of a German parachute. These were dropped with a long length of copper wire hanging down. The idea was that as they drifted down and sideways in the wind they would disrupt electricity supplies and presumably telephones by earthing them. This one had been caught earthing a hedge and no more was heard about them.

Apart from Dig for Victory, there was an abundance of slogans covering notice boards and walls. There can be little doubt the country suffered from spy mania. This was kept on the boil by posters declaring "Walls Have Ears" and "Careless Talk Costs Lives". Doubtless there were many more but those two have stuck in my memory. It would have been extremely difficult for a spy. People lived in close communities and strangers or travellers excited a deal of interest.

During the early days of the Home Guard weapons were in mighty short supply. Sporting rifles and shotguns were pressed into service. For example the Major had a pair of Mannlicher rifles designed for deer stalking. One of these resided in a gun-rack above the dining room table, the other went to Joe Dyas who farmed The Leavenhalls. Far more lethal were the boxes of ball ammunition issued to owners of 12 bores. It was stated quite clearly on the box that they were safe for use in choked barrels! All I can say is that I would have preferred to be neither user nor target bearing in mind the state of some of the old bangers they were issued for!

Looking back I really think school teachers, particularly those in primary schools, were some of the most unsung heroes of the war. Early on they had to ensure all the little dears had their gas-masks and knew where to find them throughout the day. They had to supervise gas-mask drills and air raid drills which in our case meant getting under our desks! Then the government introduced a scheme whereby every kid received a warm mug of – well Lord knows what it was – but it tasted not unlike Horlicks and was based on dried milk. All this to be dealt with, on top of the every day shortages of stationery, pencils, rubbers, coke for the boiler, light bulbs –everything! On top of all this they undertook the running of the National Savings Scheme, no mean task in itself, not to mention weekly raffles for something or other which I forget.

As hostilities continued Savings Weeks became the in thing. There were Spitfire Weeks, Battleship Weeks, you name it, we had it, and invariably the youngsters were involved in poster designing or model making competitions all of which were organised by –guess who?

Having so often heard the words since, it is tempting to imagine I can remember Churchill's speeches. Of course not, But, what I do remember, is that amazing voice and the effect it had on his audiences.

One of these speeches we listened to at Jim Coombe's, the Head Gardener. At that time they had no "electric" and their wireless, a rather splendid affair, ran from rechargeable accumulators. I recall that Jim had taken the precaution of connecting a freshly charged accumulator and the two families hung on every word Churchill uttered. Afterwards there was great merriment among the adults concerning something he had said— "Some chicken—Some neck" Believe me they had lived every word he uttered, and relived them for long enough after he finished. There can be no doubt those speeches were momentous: the shot in the arm the whole nation was longing for.

Quite early in the war the countryside around Brockton became dotted with aeroplanes, each under a convenient hedgerow tree of which there were plenty. In addition each had its canopy of camouflage netting. We were friendly with P.C.Layton and family and one evening I cycled over with him to have a look at and even inside one of the planes. A Wellington bomber, I can remember little about it apart from the diamond shaped metal framing and endless miles of wiring. There were also Blenheim fighter bombers. Local rumour later recorded they had been destined for the Middle East. Interesting to recall perhaps that cycling along the two miles or so of main road it is highly unlikely we would have seen a single motor vehicle.

Parades and military demonstrations became a feature of life; almost a highlight you could say. Shortly after the German air offensive began a Messerschmidt fighter plane which had been downed was put on display in Bridgnorth. It was displayed in the yard of the pub, I forget its name, but was where my grandfather used to stable his nag on market days. There was quite a crowd there including a fellow with a gold chain round his neck. I remember being highly impressed that Father actually knew this dignitary and spent some time chatting to him. Later he told me it was the Mayor. Every day the news bulletins concentrated on this aerial war being waged down south; numbers and details of enemy planes destroyed. By comparison our own losses always seemed surprisingly small. A figure of 183 –could it really have been that – sticks in my memory. Anyway it was the big day, the turning point as it were, and soon afterwards Goering decided to cut his losses and switch to night bombing. On the day in question, I seem to recall R.A.F. losses were in the low twenties.

Every day we kids arrived at school fully briefed with the latest score and playtime was marked by endless dogfights as we raced around, arms outstretched and imitating the roar of Merlin engines and chatter of machine guns. Pictures of planes, enemy and our own, were readily available and we knew the lot. Spitfires and Hurricanes, Wellingtons and Blenheims, Dorniers and Heinkels, Messerschmidts and Junkers, Handley Page Hampdens, Manchesters and Stukas all reeled off the tongue. Had we assimilated schoolwork a quarter as well we should have ranked with the academic elite.

I can never recall it being called the Battle of Britain, but that was what we were following. Later of course we learned that the score sheet was far different from that claimed at the time. But did it matter? Propaganda is a tool of war and the population was lapping it up. Until then the taste of success had been rare indeed.

On another occasion I was taken to see the Boulton and Paul Defiant, not unlike a Hurricane but with a revolving gun turret immediately behind the pilot's cockpit. It was designed as a night fighter and its designer owned a large house and grounds just out of Bridgnorth, Oldbury I think. Anyway that is where we went. I believe a number of Defiants were produced but the plane never made any real impact.

Parades were held in local towns. My recollections of one held in Shifnal are amazingly clear. Local Home Guard units, the Fire Service, A.R.P. and contingents from local R.A.F. and Army establishments and a local dignitary, in this case, Lord Bradford, to take the salute. I forget who provided the band, but our local Bobby, P.C. Layton led the parade, and I believe the Home Guard had actually got rifles by then. Anyway it was deemed a great success all round.

On another occasion the local Home Guard units staged a demonstration of their skills in the park surrounding a large house in Shifnal. Father was heavily involved, being in charge of both camouflage and bombing demonstrations. Blasts on a whistle resulted in fellows appearing in all sorts of places where previously there had only been trees and bushes and open field. Then the public were kept at a safe distance whilst Sticky bombs, and 75 grenades, and Molotov Cocktails as I think they were known even then, to say nothing of the Blacker Bombard all did there deadly work against simulated German targets. It was all very reassuring and that was all the public needed.

Following the Battle of Britain, for we will call it that, the population really knew it had a war on its hands. There were servicemen and women everywhere, and with lack of public transport they quickly developed the art of hitch-hiking. The beckoning thumb became a familiar sight on the roads and the few remaining motorists and lorry drivers were only too pleased to oblige.

Farm production was getting into full swing and everyone weighed in. The Major, who after World War I only had one leg, spent countless hours thistle spudding around the Park or brushing out young plantations in the woods. Tom Gray the Butler did similar work and so too Father who divided his time between helping his two or three remaining keepers with rabbit and rat control and the Home Guard which claimed most evenings and weekends for the duration.

Kynaston Lloyd was bombing officer for the area and Pa his number one. Between them they instructed not only the local Home Guard units in the throwing of Mills grenades, but also most of the local army units. Can you believe that? Since this was all done with W.W.I vintage grenades it was hardly surprising they were landed with a high proportion of "duds" which had to be destroyed with demolition charges. As you may guess life was not without the odd incident—scary at the time but amusing later. On one occasion a great strapping youth of well over six feet arrived in the throwing bay – (a sandbagged trench in the ground). He was the picture of confidence. No problem here thought Father. Sure enough the lad hurled the grenade alright. Trouble was it went up and up instead of up and forward! Realising the problem the lad turned to make a bolt for the entrance. Pa collared him whilst yelling to warn his assistant in the priming bay. He watched as the bomb descended to explode a yard or two beyond the trench."Right you can go now!" He wondered afterwards if the lad ever realised his dash for the open could well have meant death or injury.

Arriving home from school one day I found Father on the drying green with his binoculars trained on a distant aeroplane. He had received a call from P.C.Layton asking him to get the glasses out and try to identify this suspicious aircraft. I followed him into the house, all ears as he rang back and said he believed it was a Jerry. Later he received word it was indeed a reconnaissance machine which had been shot down before reaching the East coast.

Following the Luftwaffe's switch to night bombing things really moved. Searchlight and A.A. (Anti-Aircraft gun) batteries sprouted all over the place. One was stationed nearby on the Home Farm. A searchlight was installed in a sandbagged emplacement on the Near Turf and a small camp sprang up. A generator was placed on the edge of the road and at night a sentry stopped any passing traffic. One night as we were passing the sentry, who had been warming himself beside the generator appeared belatedly and Pa only caught sight of him after we had passed. Asked what he would have done had we failed to stop he replied that "He would have stuck one in us!" Next morning Father paid a little visit to the Battery Commander. After that there were no more sentries During the initial few months of the battery and pending the building of hutted accomodation the B.C., and his batman were billeted in the farmhouse with my grandparents; and the troops in a granary. Barrage balloons appeared on the skyline over the Black Country and were clearly visible as we cycled along the main road to school. On a sunny morning they fairly shone.

Early in the war the countryside was suddenly full of evacuees. Babies and toddlers arrived complete with mothers, but the majority came by themselves, with a label round their neck I believe, and were allocated to available homes on arrival. Bill Smith and his wife and young son had arrived at home some time previously their own house having been commandeered. They were long time friends and Bill, a gardener at Weston Park, who had been assigned to war work somewhere in the Black Country, spent the weekends with us. Because of this we were not allocated evacuees but my Grandmother living alone in Bridgnorth was allocated a couple of lads. They were from the rougher end of Liverpool and I often wonder who got the greater shock – them or Grannie! They were keen to go home and when she asked why they were so keen to get back to Liverpool which was being heavily bombed the reply came as a shock. "They enjoyed watching the dead'uns being collected in the mornings."

Once again the poor old school teachers were in the thick of things. On top of their existing problems they had suddenly to cope with this influx of new, completely disorientated and no doubt very disturbed youngsters. I cannot say exactly how many arrived at Norton C. of E., a school of approximately 60 or 70, but it would have been well over 20 – perhaps more. The Grammar school in Bridgnorth received a whole school – the George Dixon from Smethwick. A lot of teachers came with the evacuees, which must have created more problems, but somehow the schools coped. It must have been a strange world these kids from Liverpool and the Black Country suddenly found themselves in. Many of them had never sat down at a table to a square meal before. In some cases fish and chips and bread and Stork (margarine) appeared to have been their staple diet. They were genuinely shocked to discover milk came from cows as at home it had always come out of a bottle. Some of them, particularly the women, soon left and returned home preferring to risk the bombing, but most settled well in their new homes and some remained for the duration of the war. Their eventual departure must have been yet another wrench in their young lives.

Apley Hall had been converted as a convalescent hospital for officers. This occurred early on in the war. After being declared open it remained empty for months. Fully staffed and equipped it waited, and waited, - then suddenly the imminent arrival of a patient was hot news on the local grapevine. Oh the ironies of life! Was he wounded? Was he blazes. The poor blighter had suffered a mosquito bite which had turned septic. You can imagine the hilarity it caused in the district as, needless to say, the septic bit was always omitted!

As time passed, and the Hall filled up Mother began to provide B. and B. for wives and relatives of the inmates. Through it we met a great range of people, including Czechs, Poles and Canadians. It was a home from home for them and friendships were forged which long outlived the war. One still flourishes as I write -55 years on!

Timber, like food, had become a national priority and from an early stage of the war timber felling became a major activity across the countryside. To begin with the Estate woodmen, with their ancient wooden wheeled timber carriage, were the sole operators. A row of elms up Cheswardine Lane were the first to go. Soon the Estate stalwarts were replaced by small teams of timber fellers. Trees were faced out at the base with an axe and then a cross-cut saw was put to work. With a man at each end they worked kneeling down with the cutting edge towards them. It looked awkward but judging by the rate at which the trees came down was highly efficient. Bear in mind that chain saws were as yet unavailable.

Once the fellers were finished another gang arrived. Usually three in number they lived in a caravan and "tushed" (dragged) out the "sticks" (trunks) with a crawler tractor and then loaded them onto timber carriages. Using the crawler they could get the carriages across land which horses, or even the carriage tractor unit, would not even look at. Apart from the old steam ploughing and threshing engines it was the first time anybody had ever seen real mechanical power on the land—a foretaste of things to come?

Away from the country and back to the towns and suddenly it felt

as though everywhere was being bombed. When the Black Country was catching it we could hear it plainly and on many occasions, notably the Coventry blitz could see the glow in the sky. Bear in mind there was the blackout so any illumination was easy to spot.

Air raid sirens wailing the "Alert" and with a single continuous note for the "All Clear" became the norm as did the noise of German bombers overhead. They had a characteristic engine noise, a sort of pulsing sound quite unlike British or American planes.

We always knew whether it was the Black Country or Liverpool which was going to catch it. Their turning point was directly overhead and they either turned for the Midlands or continued on up the Severn for Merseyside.

My uncle (Ted) had given up his home in the Via Gellia and moved into Sheffield for the duration. His employers, Wilson by name, owned the famous Spear and Jackson tool factory and Uncle took charge of the Civil Defence there. One night during the blitz his lodgings received a direct hit. Fortunately for him he was out at the time, but was left literally with what "he stood up in". Happily the other occupants were in air raid shelters and also escaped with their lives. I well recall the hustle at home as two huge brown paper parcels of clothes and anything else which might be useful were assembled and despatched.

Just after dawn one summer's morning, as he was leaving the house, Father heard what he thought was a German plane. He popped up onto the drying green to get a better view. He was well rewarded. It was a

Jerry alright, flying so low up the valley, that he was actually looking down on it. He could see every last detail, the pilot, the gunner, right down to the rivets in the fuselage Dashing inside he reported the sighting by telephone but unlike the earlier spotting nothing more was ever heard.

It was during this period odd sticks of bombs fell in the surrounding countryside. One evening Mother and Father walked to the Home Farm to take the milk can and call on Grandparents. I was left with Lill Smith and young Raymond. We were somewhere upstairs and there were German aircraft overhead. Suddenly there was the whistle of bombs falling. No doubt about what it was. Mother had told me earlier that the tail fins on German bombs were designed to maximise the noise. Whether true or not I have no idea, though I believe it is true they fitted air driven sirens to their Stuka dive bombers

Strangely enough I can recall little else. Possibly the house did shake but it was certainly nothing dramatic which is surprising as the nearest bomb fell within a hundred yards. Two more dropped either side of the road by the Long Pool and two or three more in the Spring Coppice. Next day bomb disposal experts arrived on the scene and stated they had not exploded. To be fair to them there was hardly any crater to see. Father explained to them they had gone into deep clay and in a day or so the surface would collapse and form craters. He had seen the same thing with heavy shells in Belgium. I recall the riot act was read to me in no uncertain terms regarding the distance I would keep away from "the holes". How right he was. In no time the surface around them collapsed, in one case pulling down a poor old cow and killing her. Soon I was finding bits of bomb shrapnel all over the place so some had managed to find its way out.

On another occasion a bomb, I am sure it was the only one, fell over the river at Astley Abbots probably a mile distant. I was in bed and you can take it from me – that one really shook the house. It occurred during a long dry spell and next morning we found it had shaken every last piece of moss off the roof. There were barrow- fulls to clear up. A few weeks later a large patch of ceiling, all of a hundredweight, fell down in my parents bedroom.

One night the Worfe Coppice received a thorough plastering with incendiary bombs. Fortunately that was not a dry time and they burned themselves out without doing any damage. Another lot fell on Sutton Wood about the same time.

Considering its proximity to the Black Country, it is amazing Bridgnorth was bombed but once. As I recall only two or three bombs landed. A house on the little road between High Street and St. Leonard's Close was hit and two elderly ladies were killed. On hearing the news one pious lady was heard to remark- "What a blessing it didn't fall on that beautiful church!"

All manner of reasons were advanced to explain these random attacks. They had tried for the searchlight battery; the Home Farm chimney had made it look like a factory; the suspension bridge at Linley are some which spring to mind. Father's explanation was more simple and probably nearer the truth. The odd bomber crew decided to dump their load and get the hell out of it!

It rings true because though I cannot recall a single thing about them our anti-aircraft defences must have been getting steadily more effective as the blitz waned over one city after another and finally fizzled out. In the end it was reduced to the odd hit and run raid.

One thing which completely mystified the grownups, and certainly disappointed us youngsters was the searchlight battery at the Home Farm. After some months the original light was replaced by a far larger and more powerful model. At one stage a Bofors anti-aircraft gun was sited there. There were training sessions involving searchlights from neighbouring batteries. Target aircraft were picked up and pinpointed by intersecting beams. All very impressive, but never at any stage of the bombing were the lights –let alone the Bofors- used against enemy aircraft. It was a total mystery!

As the raids over here gradually finished we became increasingly aware of retaliation in the opposite direction." Last night our bombers were again in action over Germany", or similar words became an increasingly regular feature of the morning bulletins. Twin engined Wellingtons were used in small numbers. I suspect their effect was minimal but it had the grownups rubbing their hands. At last Hitler was getting a taste of his own medicine. I vividly recall one bulletin which gave an account of one crewman who had climbed out onto the wing of a stricken Wellington and had extinguished a fire in an engine! Not surprisingly he had been awarded the V.C. It would have been about this time a Wellington bomber crash landed on my uncle's farm at Alveley. One crew member was badly injured; the others walked out.

Suitable buildings in rural areas were used for storing essentials away from the risk of bombing. With its magnificent range of buildings the Home Farm was selected as a flour store. Every Sunday morning a little procession of lorries arrived laden with flour. Electric hoists were installed and bags of flour filled the granaries from floor to ceiling. Lord knows how many tons they held but it must have been hundreds. Once full to capacity the Sunday shuttle became a two way affair bringing the newly milled and removing the older flour.

During the early part of the war the Home Guard were given the task of acting as lookouts at night. Exactly how long this went on for I am not sure but certainly for a year or so, presumably as long as invasion or airborne landings by spies or paratroops was considered a threat. What I do know is that for guys expected to do a full day's work both before and after their night "on" this would have been tiring in the extreme. A team of six or eight if I remember correctly assembled nightly. In a platoon of 40 this would have worked out at every 4th or 5th night "on". To begin with their observation post was a small wooden hut on Windmill Hill. After a few months they moved to the comparative luxury of an attic in Stockton rectory where they used the flat roof as O.P. and the lead guttering as a urinal –But that is another story.

Being a firm believer in good shooting Father got permission to build a rifle range in the Park. This was used not only by the home team but by Home Guard units across a wide area. His own team he trained to an amazingly high standard and when Western Command held a competition in which over 800 teams took part they went on to win the final. It was an event developed by the army and the home team, which included a sixty year old farmer, one Jack Bowen, beat the pre-war record established by one of the Guards regiments! Mighty embarrassing for the military brass assembled who, sportsmen to a man, declared the record had only been equalled. Never mind, Dad's Army went home with a smile on its face albeit a trifle unsteady on its feet! They returned to the more mundane duties of impeding the army on its manoeuvres. This time the attack was from the South and Pa posted two likely lads as lookouts along the main road. Time went by and with no sign of the invading horde Syd and Dick decided a bite of lunch would not come amiss. It turned out they had been spotted and two enterprising Tommies slipped round behind them unseen. Lunch was interrupted when these lads informed Syd and Dick they were now prisoners! The reply must have come as a shock. "Well for your information you buggers are supposed to be coming from that direction, so you can bloody sod off and try the proper way!"

Another news bulletin remains firmly in my mind. It was the announcement of the final break-through at El Alamein. Pa roused the household and we all sat glued to the radio to hear it repeated, "The Axis forces in North Africa are in full retreat".

Arrival of the Americans or Yanks as we called them brought a whole new dimension to our world. They constructed camps locally and this involved carting large quantities of what I can only think was fly-ash from Buildwas power station. We soon realised they did not do things by halves. Used as we were to the British convoys creeping along at snail's pace, - two of us once managed to race one from Bridgnorth to Norton on our bikes- these boys fairly buzzed along.

Their lorries were something else too. Great long bonnets, they appeared vastly overpowered, with wheels and axles all over the place. Their bumper bars were built to stop a tank which was perhaps as well as the local hedges soon began to take a battering. By the end of hostilities I doubt whether there was a one hundred yard length of hedge left intact between Norton and Bridgnorth.

One frosty morning as we stood and watched outside the village school a solitary jeep with four occupants buzzed past. Then to our amazement, on a straight stretch of empty road, he managed to drive up the hedge bank and tip the little beggar onto its side. The four of them picked themselves up apparently unharmed and even less concerned. They were obviously four strong lads because they managed to push it back onto its wheels. Then in they climbed and away they went!

But to return to the carting of fly-ash. With petrol scarce we were used to seeing lorries running fully laden with not an ounce of carrying capacity unused. For this ash they would have been using high side boards. Not so the Yanks. Petrol apparently was no problem as they whizzed back and forth, their loads not one fifth of what their powerful lorries would have been capable.

Never mind we soon got the hang of standing at the roadside and yelling "Any Gum Chum?" Occasionally we were rewarded, even on one or two occasions, with a packet of Camel cigarettes. Rumour had it that their tobacco contained dung of the animal on the packet! A feature of all American convoys, large or small, was the breakdown wagon which invariably brought up the rear. Their ability to drive vehicles through hedges, even really heavy stuff, really was nigh unbelievable. Cycling to school one morning a tank carrier and its load were on their sides in one of the Leavenhall fields. That lot we said was going to take a bit of shifting. To our amazement it had all gone when we cycled back that afternoon.

With the arrival of the Yanks Saturday nights in wartime Bridgnorth were greatly enlivened. On two occasions G.S. wagons with full loads of revellers took a short cut from the New Road to Underhill Street. This involved driving through a wall and dropping Lord knows how many feet to the road below. On each occasion the wagon landed on its wheels. There was the odd broken arm, otherwise no loss of life. Quite, quite unbelievable!

There were also the inevitable brawls at least one of which ended in fatalities from knifings. My first insight into racial tension.

Apart from the arrival of the Yanks so many other things were happening. For one thing all sorts of new aeroplanes were appearing in the sky. British Beaufighters and Mosquitoes, both twin engined, Halifaxes, Stirlings, and Lancasters, great four engined machines began to appear.

Following the early raids by the Wellingtons the bombing of Germany built up at an amazing pace. These new four-engined machines notably the Lancs took over the job and soon we were hearing of 500 and finally 1000 bomber raids by night.

News bulletins spoke of Stalingrad and then we knew Hitler was being pushed back on two fronts. American planes were appearing in numbers. Flying Fortresses, Martin Marauders, Lockheed Hudsons, the Forts sometimes flying in huge formations escorted by Mustangs and twin engined, twin fusalaged fighters which I think were called Lockheed Lightnings. Soon the Yanks were adding to the bombardment of Germany with 1000 bomber daylight raids.

In addition Dakotas began to appear in number, and not long after that they and Whitley bombers were to be seen towing gliders, the glider always flying a few feet higher than the aircraft towing it. Soon all these planes began to sport black and white stripes on their wings and all the military vehicles had a white star inside a white circle painted on roofs and bonnets. All this we were informed was to aid recognition of friendly forces.

As we got older we were increasingly able to follow the course of events. We followed the news of the Battle of the Atlantic (war against U-boats), helped no doubt by the film shown at the Majestic. Just as well none of us were old enough to be able to realise what a close run thing it was.

As the Eighth Army swept across North Africa, then invaded Sicily and Italy numbers of Italian and German PoW's (Prisoners of War) began to appear and made a useful addition to the workforce on local farms Our searchlight battery was decommissioned and became an Italian PoW. camp. Initially they were clad in chocolate coloured denims with a red circular patch sown in the back. All this for easy recognition in case they attempted to escape. That was quickly dropped as it became rapidly apparent all they wanted was a quiet life until the end of the war.

By this stage the news was usually cheering. There were the odd set-backs. One morning following a massive raid it was announced the R.A.F. had lost 70 bombers over Nuremberg (Later we learned the real count was 90) Father explained how serious it was. If losses continued on that scale the bombing effort could not be sustained. Clearly tactics were revised and the bombing continued with much lighter losses. We began to hear about Pathfinders and the Dambuster Raid created a wave of national euphoria!

Typhoon fighters joined the host of aircraft and we learned they were for "tank busting" with rockets. Meanwhile the build-up of army convoys grew apace. One day an excited youngster caused a stir in the playground by shouting "There were boats on wheels!" He was right too. Our first of many convoys of American amphibious vehicles, D.U.K.W.s or something of that nature. Anyway we knew them as "DUCKS" and so did everyone else.

Tanks too were appearing in numbers, usually on carriers, but sometimes self propelled. Cats eyes had been invented and were installed along the main road. A convoy of tanks came through and took the lot out. That was the end of them for the duration!

At this stage I was cycling to the Grammar school, along with several others. Looking back what a worry that must have been for our parents. The Yanks drove at speed and their driving was atrocious. Fred Lane and Tom Gray were both knocked off their bikes but escaped injury. I only had one near squeak. Approaching the tight bend at the bottom of Newton Bank at speed I realised a gravel lorry had shed some of its load making the surface a skid pan. As usual we were being overtaken by a convoy and a big wagon was bearing down on me fast. Providentially there was a junction on the bend and knowing there was no way I was going to negotiate it without ending on the road in front of the wagon, I managed to swing into the side road. On sober reflection I knew that had been a narrow squeak. Another thing about the Yanks. They had an irritating habit of standing on the running board of their wagons to relieve themselves. Anything in the way, and we sometimes were,- too bad!

One sunny day I was walking across the Lodge Field. A plane was passing over and suddenly there was a brilliant flash of light on its fuselage. It was not repeated and I convinced myself it must have been caused by reflection of sunlight. Walking on across the turf, I was suddenly aware of flashes of light above me. It was somewhat scary until I realised my vision had not gone haywire but what I was seeing was the reflection of sunlight from strips of highly polished metal foil twisting and turning as it floated down. Relief! Soon I was collecting them from all over the field and had dozens of pieces. After that we had several more scatterings involving different shapes and sizes. Later we learnt it was a counter-measure against German radar and we had been watching experiments to determine the best combination.

On another occasion we were picking potatoes opposite the Deersheds in the Park when two aircraft flew over. One was a fighter, the other a bomber, what types I completely forget. Anyway the bomber had a huge round hole in one wing and an engine out of action. It has always been a mystery to me. Why over Shropshire so far from the main bomber bases and what one wonders was the final fate of crew and pilot?

Mention of spud picking or "bashing" as we called it takes me back to farming. One day, late on in the war, a brand new Oliver combine arrived at the Home Farm. On our usual Sunday morning walk I tackled Grandfather about this for he had never been in favour of combines. He explained – very patiently- that his workforce was getting very tired. Several of his main men were getting on in years and they could not maintain the present work rate for ever. The combine would help see them through to the end of the war and after that it would have to go. He went on to explain the weakness of the combine was that all the rubbish (weed seed) went straight back on the land. How was he to know that selective weed killers were being developed, and they, together with the combine, would revolutionise farming

But I digress. Back to the war, or at least my recollections of it. We have come to the stage when everyone knew the invasion of Europe was imminent. Our main road, winding, twisty old thing that it was, was the principle route from Liverpool to the South Coast. Military traffic built up until it was running night and day. Tanks were being transported by the thousand, Stewarts the light ones, Grants and of course Shermans the main battle tank. At 35-40 tons most were carried singly but the Yanks brought over some colossal transporters capable of taking three light or two heavies at a time. Their cabs were enormous, with cooking and sleeping facilities for the off-duty crew. It was said the only time they ever stopped was to load or take on fuel. Probably true because they passed through the village with a new cargo every day for weeks on end. Getting from Liverpool to the South Coast and back every 24 hours on the roads as they were then was some feat.

After going to bed one night there was a terrific noise of aircraft overhead. Pa and Mother came into the room and drew back the curtains. As we stood watching the sky seemed full of green navigation lights. Whether towing gliders or not is impossible to say but we surmised they were troop transporters practicing night flying. This was repeated on two or three nights.

A few mornings later we were roused with the news of the invasion. On getting to school it was again announced at Morning Prayers (Assembly) by Joey Barret our head master. This was it! The moment we had all been waiting for. It's a certain fact none of us youngsters and indeed few of the grownups, realised what a fantastic, or indeed precarious feat, it really was. Listening to the news reports it all seemed so easy. A few days later "Fuzzy" Stokes came to school and announced his uncle had won the V.C. Occasionally, very occasionally, the head master announced the death of a former pupil at prayers. Those rows of names from 1914-18 which took up a large area of wall in the library were not, thank God, going to be repeated.

Conscientious objectors had a much easier ride during the second world war than the first. My parents explained to me that some people held strong and genuine convictions on moral grounds. They, indeed most people, had no difficulty with that so long as they were prepared to do their bit in non-combative roles. Many of them did just that and indeed undertook highly dangerous occupations such as sick-birth attendants on merchant ships. There were others though for whom it was the easy option. One in particular ran a shop in Bidgnorth at considerable profit and that caused a lot of bad feeling locally.

One morning in the later stages of the conflict Joey Barret

announced at Prayers that the senior classes would be attending a cinema show that afternoon. They duly went, and on their return we less privileged juniors naturally wanted to hear what it had all been about. Not a thing could we extract from them They had been sworn to secrecy and their secret they kept.

Most of our parents attended the same film over the next few days. They too were loathe to talk, but gradually it was explained to us, not in any graphic detail I may assure you, but enough for us to realise that Hitler and his Nazis had committed a hitherto unsuspected and quite horrific crime against humanity. It was years I believe before most of us realised the full and awful implications of the Death Camps.

Some time before, or was it soon after D-Day we began to hear about flying bombs, or Doodle- bugs as they were nick-named. Officially called the VI (V One) they were rocket propelled pilotless air craft packed with a considerable load, (1000 lbs.), as I recall, of high explosive. Fired from launching sites across the Channel they came over in considerable numbers and caused great damage where they fell. They were highly inaccurate and so were aimed at large populated regions in the South East. They could only be defined as weapons designed to cause terror among the civilian population

Many were shot down by Ack Ack (i.e. Anti-aircraft) batteries and fighter aircraft. Then it was found that a really fast fighter, say a Mk. IX Spitfire could fly alongside and by lifting its wing tip under that of the Doodle bug could tip it to fall short of its target. Fortunately they had a limited range and the advance across France soon robbed them of their launching sites.

VIs were superseded by VIIs. These were proper rockets – the real thing!

Too fast for anti-aircraft fire or fighters to deal with, and with much greater range and payload they were launched from sites in Holland or Germany itself. I cannot recall how many actually landed. With total air superiority it was a question of seeking out and destroying their launching sites until they could be overrun.

There was considerable rumour about a VIII. What prompted it I have no idea. For one thing it was a logical progression. For another there had long been talk of the super bomb.

There came the point when everyone knew the war against Germany was in its final stages. Daily maps in the papers showed German occupied territory, and then Germany itself, becoming ever smaller, the area of liberated Europe ever larger. With VIs and VIIs out of the reckoning the A.R.P. seemed redundant. So too the Home Guard. Their last real job, and it had proved a mighty time consuming one had been the marking and labelling of equipment destined for the D Day landings and subsequent supply. By now though it had become something of a social club. Certainly as time went on, and victory ever more certain, it was surprising how many "celebrations" they managed to organise dinners for!

Out in the playground one dinner hour some comedian reported a plane without any propellers! Unfortunately for him he did so in the hearing of Swann the maths master who was never at a loss for the odd pithy remark. Perhaps fortuitously, and just in time to save him the full treatment, the Gloucester Meteor completed another tight circuit. Now who had the laugh? For we all stood and gawped in amazement as we watched our first jet whistle over. (The test pilot was Jim Cooksey, son of a local family - hence our free display)

Soon afterwards we saw a second type. This had a single jet engine in a short fuselage. Twin booms extended from the wings to its wide tailplane, just like the American Lightnings. If I recall correctly they were called Vampires.

About the same time we heard the Germans had developed a jet plane. A couple of years earlier that would have been serious. Now we knew it was unimportant For we were well aware they were finished. American and British armies were advancing almost unopposed: the Russians had taken Berlin. Everyone knew it was over, and yet when the announcement of the surrender to Montgomery on Luneberg Heath was finally broadcast ---it still seemed unbelievable!

What we youngsters had expected I really do not know. I do know there were massive and prolonged celebrations everywhere. In our village a Sports Day was organised for the afternoon, with a bonfire and a dance to follow in the evening. Father was given the honour of lighting the bonfire. Yet somehow it was muted. There was still Japan to deal with and Lord knows what horrors to follow in that sphere.

All attention was now focused on the war in the Pacific. The 14th Army, the Forgotten Army as it had become known was suddenly in the news. Then as the world seemed to be taking stock, snatching a breather as it were, before finally deciding how best to settle Japan, the problem was suddenly no more! It evaporated with the unleashing of two atomic bombs!

So now we celebrated V-J Day. More sports, another bonfire on the school field and more celebrations. This time it was for real! A massive victory parade was held in London. Thousands made the journey to watch it. Millions more trooped to watch it a day or so later at their local cinema. His Home Guard duties finished, his platoon got together and presented Father with a beautiful little rosewood table. He had surely earned it and we still treasure it

4. All Is Safely Gathered In

"Give us this day our daily bread."

When did any of us, living as we do in this well fed land of ours, last intone that line of the Lord's Prayer ----- and really mean it?

Well take a stroll with me, back across the years, to a time when I was but knee –high to a grasshopper. Come back to the gathering darkness of an October evening during the early Forties. Watch with me the good folk of the parish making their way uphill from the village and from all the outlying cottages and farmsteads. They are leaving blacked-out homes to cross a blacked-out landscape to a blacked-out church. No bells peal, for until this war is over, they will only ring out to warn of invasion.

Once inside though we are in another world. That venerable door of studded oak rattles and creaks repeatedly to swell our numbers, which go on swelling till every pew is packed. For, you see, it is Harvest Festival. And now there is even the sound of folding chairs being set out in the aisle.

As the church continues to fill noise increases, more creaking and scraping of chairs, shuffling of feet, buzz of muted conversation, solemn music from the organ; and everyone exchanging but one opinion - how wonderful the old building looks. Wonderful indeed! Quite beautiful in fact, for it is like being inside a cornucopia - an architectural cornucopia!

Sheaves of wheat and oats, ancient symbols of fertility, line the walls of the porch and surround the font to provide a golden backdrop to displays of great marrows and pumpkins, onions, carrots and parsnips,

huge swedes and mangolds, all interspersed with stunning arrangements of dahlias, chrysanths and michaelmas-daisies, never failing
stalwarts of farmhouse and cottage gardens.

But listen now! The organ has stopped. And behind us none too
successful efforts are being made to stifle the sounds of mirth generated
by some wag commenting, "Old so and so shouldner be 'ere---Well
should 'ee now if 'ee's still got eight acre of ruddy wheat to lug?" Choir-
boys hidden behind the screen, now brilliantly transformed into a riot
of Autumn colour, reluctantly abstain from buzzing small objects at
each other. A reverential hush is descending as Vicar comes forward;
the only sounds still audible are the lad giving the organ a final few
pumps and a sparrow chirping in the roof. Vicar waits, and now at long

last, total silence reigns; it seems both lad and sparrow have finally got the message! His point made Vicar announces the first hymn.

"We plough the fields and scatter—" The sheer volume of sound which erupts from the packed congregation is exhilarating. Everyone in the parish must surely have squeezed in here, everyone of course except the young men and women away at the war. As we sing folk gaze about them and admire displays of Majestic and King Edward potatoes vying for space in the window alcoves with Blenheim and Bramley, Pippin, Cox and Russet apples.

Behind the Squire, ensconced front left, are seated the tenants, and behind the vicar's family, pewed front right, are ranged the Estate staff. All nicely graded, their place in the local hierarchy demarked by their proximity to the front, or viewed from another standpoint --- the back!

Anyway the old hymn is getting our service away to a rattling fine start. George Sherwood, a mighty nasal tenor, the brass section of the choir as it were, is establishing his customary dominance. Once our George has settled on a top note he takes a bit of dislodging, but his antics are well known ---and catered for! Organist waits, choir pauses, congregation take a breather, Vicar casts a glance heavenwards, then----away we all go again!

Usually, and I may as well confess it, the unmitigated tedium of the Church of England litany bores me stiff. But here now, with so much to gaze around at and borne along on waves of rousing sound, it seems no time at all before Vicar is disappearing behind a screen of floral decoration which was once the wrought iron railing to the pulpit steps. He reappears to peep out at us from on high above a thicket of trailing greenery and Autumn foliage.

This then is the dreaded moment. True the Guinness Book of Records has yet to be launched, but were that not the case, rest assured the length and tedium of Vicar's sermons would guarantee him pole position. Today though –Glory be – there is so much else to distract. For instance that eye-catching flower arrangement around the lectern, an array of hot-house flowers no less, product of a conspiracy between the Head Gardener from the Hall and Vicar's good lady. But hush! No way must those officials from the Food Ministry get to hear about this one!

At last, almighty long last, the sermon ends and not even George can disrupt the surging, welling tempo as organist, choir and congregation combine to send the triumphal notes and words of the Great Harvest Hymn crashing and reverberating amongst the rafters.

"All is safely gathered in!" Simple the words--. Mighty their meaning; the difference between feast and famine,--- between victory and defeat! Scarce a soul in this church packed with farming folk is not involved with food production. Well they know, that by the grace of God, we are blessed yet again with another bountiful wartime harvest.

"All is safely gathered in!" Sing the words again, and again, louder yet louder; for what better way can there be for expressing this thanksgiving for which we are gathered

Service ended we file out with Vicar's final blessing ringing in our ears. Meanwhile Mother has to quietly explain why a certain farmer friend is exclaiming—"He will not come in to the damn place never again!" Just as well perhaps he is in "The place" or damn could well have been something else! Anyway it would appear Vicar has mortally offended him by seizing on the occasion to point out there are fifty one other Sabbaths in the year. Poor old Vicar. Never was a man over-blessed with tact.

As we troop out through the door a huge Harvest moon is climbing into a clear night sky; the parish lantern to light our way home. Someone voices aloud what many are thinking, "The poor old Black Country could cop it again tonight". Meanwhile the older choristers, having checked that the younger choristers have not let the wind out of their tyres, are grabbing their bikes from against the churchyard wall. Moon and Black Country are the last thing on their minds. They are headed for yet another place of worship, one where the prayer books have handles

So there lies your answer. When German U-boats stalked the Atlantic, and their bombers blasted our ports, when food was rationed, and the spectre of real starvation hovered on the horizon--- That then oh ye of full bellies, and little faith, was when "Give us this day our daily bread" was last spoken with real meaning!

5. Deer Shooting Days

There used to be a herd of fallow deer in Apley Park and every year there was a cull to control numbers. When the war began, and that was before I was old enough to watch the shooting, the entire herd which had for so long graced the park had to go. Well not quite, for a little bunch of eight or nine escaped through a gap made by a storm blown tree falling across the deer fencing. They certainly took full advantage of their good fortune surviving in the woods throughout the war years.

Does were usually shot by keepers using twelve bores with large shot, certainly not less than BB. Bucks were selectively killed by stalking with a rifle the object being to leave the best specimens thereby gradually improving the quality of the herd. Even though I never watched the actual shooting, those deer culling days are firmly implanted in my memory. A horse drawn game cart arrived in the yard and unloaded the day's kill at the slaughter house door. Then it was all systems go, first skinning then hanging carcases on wooden gambrels to finish dressing out. There were no white smocks or hats to be seen, just keepers in working togs, boots and leggings, shirt sleeves,waistcoats and cloth caps. Your modern day hygienist would have had apoplexy. What there was though was cold water aplenty, a running tap filling a zinc tank whilst the slaughter house itself was spotless.

A deep hole would have been dug in the nearby pit hole and entrails and trimmings were wheel barrowed to it for burial. Skinning and dressing out completed, and that could take some time, the keepers could step back and assess their handiwork: a result any professional slaughterman would have been happy to call his own. Then they set off for home, each with a package of liver for themselves and offal for their dogs, all wrapped in the newspaper which had held their lunches. Newspaper you exclaim? Yes newspaper, the same which folk always used to eat their fish and chips out of.

Whilst the skinning and dressing out was being done, someone or two would have been stretching out and nailing deerskins on the side of a long wooden building. Once thoroughly dried they were rolled up and sold to the leather trade. Doeskin gloves were much in vogue for fashionable ladies; perhaps they still are. As for the carcases, a few were sold locally and others retained for use at the Hall or donated to hospitals; whether eaten by patients or medics was never enquired. Most though went to game dealers.

No! They did not travel in refrigerated transport. Once thoroughly cooled they were wrapped and sown up in hessian – I still have the old bagging needle which came in useful for sowing up wool sacks. Rolls of a really fine woven hessian were bought for the job; then it was back on the game cart, which would have been scrubbed out again, and down to catch an early train at Linley station. That venison would have been in Birmingham, Manchester even London the same day!

6. Stockton-Norton C Of E School

First day at school. At that time it happened on your fifth birthday –or surely it would have been the day after? Anyway there I was riding on the carrier seat of my mother's bicycle with vocal encouragement coming from Mrs. Jones of the corner cottage.—" Oh so you're off for a bit of cane then?" Judging from the relish in her voice she clearly thought I would be the better for it! That afternoon I walked the mile and a half home, not having had the cane, but having met a young fellow who was to become a life-long friend. Fully a month my senior and clearly well versed in scholastic affairs he had taught me a little rhyme. Insy-Winsy spider. Proudly I recited it to my parents.Unfortunately instead of finishing " Washed the spider out" my newly acquired gem concluded with – " washed the bugger out". I can only imagine my parents had a job to keep their faces straight but to their eternal credit were successful in doing so and remonstrated appropriately.

Doubtless they concluded their little fellow was off to a flier!

After that first day it was a question of walking to school until I was considered old enough to ride a bike. That would have been when I was seven or eight, or perhaps to be more accurate when a bike could be obtained for they were nigh impossible to get hold of during the war.

Of the educational side I really can not remember a deal –so what is new you say? Anyway we learned twice times tables, thrice times tables and every other table off by heart, and then of course there was learning to read. To this day I can still recollect the twenty six little pictures ranged around the classroom walls. First an apple with a big "A" and a small "a". Then a bat with a big "B" and a small "b" and so on through the alphabet. Brilliant! C—A—T and D—O—G, you could almost work it out for yourself – and most of us did. I am told the latest educational wizardry advocates a not dissimilar approach.

Then of course there was religion. At a C. of E school that featured well up on the curriculum. It damn near was the curriculum. Prayers and a hymn got the school day off to a flier. Singing lessons were a must if only to supply new voices for the church choir. Lunch was preceded by a sung grace and followed by a sung, a sung what? Really I do'nt know what it was and no cleric I have ever asked has ever been able to provide the answer. Was it a thanksgiving or perhaps a stimulant to continued erudition. Who knows! For the infants a bible story always preceded " Home Time". Then of course there were commandments, assorted psalms and hymns to learn by heart.

Thursday mornings the parson came in for an hour; at least that is what it seemed like. He was a nice old boy, but took his duty seriously, never failing to remind us a place in heaven awaited good little boys but anything less could land you well and truly in the mire i.e. a most unpleasant spot. Why not little girls I wondered? They appeared quite immune from these strictures.

And of course we were encouraged not to aim too high in life. Blessed are the lowly; Blessed are the meek; The first shall be last and the last shall be first. Then of course that glorious verse now omitted from "All Things Bright and Beautiful".

The rich man in his castle
The poor man at his gate
The good Lord in his heaven
Ordered their estate.

Interpret as you will; it was pure unashamed social brainwashing, but frankly I know it went clean over our heads and had not the slightest effect on any of us.

Of course we were tested in religious knowledge and received certificates if we made the grade I still have mine, also my mother's. Such was my proficiency in the subject I was actually awarded the top accolade – a prayer book. These awards were handed out before break time on the morning of Ascension Day. Then we all crocodiled half a mile up hill to the church for a service after which we were free to go home.

There were two other days of note in the school calendar. Oak Apple day always got off to a riotous start. Custom dictated pupils should arrive with an oak apple and bunch of nettles. Bearers of apples were supposed to be immune from attack by nettles. Somehow that message never seemed to get through. As usual lesser boys always ended up being chased by larger boys. All that can be said in favour of the larger boys was that the British sense of fair play demanded that apples be removed from lesser boys before nettling them.

Then there was Empire Day. Our head mistress hung a large map atop the blackboard and unrolled it with due ceremony. There displayed before us lay the empire on which the sun never set. Looking back I know those great swathes of pink really did ring a bell and were a cause of considerable pride. Tribalism runs deep and is an easily aroused human emotion. Of course the royal family got a favourable mention and the king in particular always emerged with image enhanced.

Apart from the parson there were other regular visitors to the school. One was the attendance officer. Having checked the attendance register Daddy Rhodes went in search of any unexplained absentees. By all accounts he invariably put the fear of God up both them and their mamas. Our district nurse conducted nit hunts on a regular basis and a school doctor and dentist visited annually.A schools inspector also put in the odd appearance.

Hand writing was taken very seriously. We were not allowed pen and ink until we left the infant class. Every pupil then had a little china ink well and a pen with a nice scratchy nib. We spent hours practicing individual letters before finally being allowed to join them into words. Copper plate was the holy grail. Anyone trying to decipher my writing now might be forgiven for wondering where I featured in the proceedings.

Now what about the inner man? For my first few years kids who lived in the village went home at dinner time. For those living further afield it was a case of carrying their lunch to school. In my last year a meal was provided, presumably with County Council backing. It was prepared by two ladies from the village—and it was superb. Looking back on the facilities available to those two good souls, and then comparing what they served up with the best efforts of so much we see today, it leaves much food for thought.

There were separate playgrounds for boys and girls. Best described as a kind of gravelly texture they were dust bowls in dry weather and mud holes in wet. Winter frost turned them into skating rinks and we had great fun making slides. Toilet facilities might best be described as basic. Housed beneath a single roof, the boys had one half and the girls the other. There was a potchet sink and cold tap which was seldom guaranteed to work. When in need of the facilities the head mistress and her assistants had to use the girls side. A wall, it must have been at least six feet, divided the two sides. I mention it because my good friend of Insy- Winsy fame achieved the nigh unbelievable feat of peeing over it. He did it once too often though when the head mistress happened to be in residence.

Which leads me, not surprisingly, to the subject of corporal punishment. Yes. The cane was still in use, not by any stretch of the imagination on the scale of my father's schooldays, but quite enough to form a nice solid base for the maintenance of law and order in the classroom. Indeed one might argue for the maintenance of standards generally; and standards did not allow for irrigating such a rare plant as the head mistress. So my poor old Insy Winsy friend duly got his come-uppance!

Finally perhaps I should mention there was a war on during my time at the village school. Emergency measures and the difficulties that it brought are described in some detail under the heading "Wartime Recollections". Needless to say it did create a mountain of extra work, indeed a real challenge for our teachers – and they responded quite splendidly.

7. Bulls Eye

The gentleman who told me this story had grown up on the family farm where he and his two brothers spent many a happy hour after the rabbits with ferret and gun. On one well remembered occasion his brothers made him a little bet. Simple enough. All he had to do to collect the money was drop his trousers and let them take a pot at his bare backside from a range of forty yards. As a sporting concession lead shot in the twelve bore cartridge was to be replaced with wheat grains. Common sense urged caution, but never a lad to refuse a bet, especially if the odds were attractive enough, he entered into the spirit of the occasion.

"Did it sting a bit?" I enquired innocently.

"Sting a bit? I'll tell you what my lad! Getting your arse peppered with wheat at forty yards is a bloody painful experience. I hardly sat down for a blasted week!"

8. Wash Day

Wash Day! What Day? What the devil I hear you ask was a wash day? Well for a start it was a ritual shrouded in the mists, or should we say the steam of time. For one thing it always had to be a Monday and if nothing else it got the week away to a flier.

In our household it began at 5 a.m. when Father got up and lit a fire beneath the "copper". What, you ask was a "copper"? The "copper" was in fact an overgrown iron pudding basin built into brickwork above a cast-iron fire box. Perhaps at some stage some really were made from copper but I can never recollect seeing one. When not in use it resided beneath a very solid wooden lid. Whilst the fire was getting to grips with the "kindling" he turned a highly polished brass tap and filled the "copper" with several gallons of rain water from the "soft water" tank in the roof space. As the water gradually came to the boil it gave off a quite distinctive but by no means unpleasant aroma generated no doubt from a healthy lacing of bird droppings and rotting vegetable matter off the roof.

Mother put in an appearance at 6.30 a.m. and just as we were finishing breakfast a lovely lady called Polly Oliver arrived and sat down to a cup of tea. Having walked a mile and a half from the village come rain, hail or shine she was probably ready for one. Polly always wore the same shiny black hat secured by long hat-pins, carried the same shiny black carrier bag and arrived nicely primed with the local gossip!

Preliminaries completed the real business of the day began. Bars of soap, packets of soap-flakes, Lux I think those were called, patent soap powders guaranteed wondrous in their efficiency, soap suds up to their elbows, Mother and Polly were scarcely visible as they soaked and rinsed, pounded, scrubbed and dollied away shrouded in clouds of steam.

A zinc coated dolly tub vied for floor space with zinc coated baths. Packets of Robins Starch and cubes of Reckitts Blue appeared and added their magic to proceedings whilst really obdurate stains and dirty collars were getting their come-uppance twixt scrubbing brush and draining board. And all the time that old "copper" carried on filling the scullery with steam

Washing, scrubbing, dollying, rinsing, completed the next job was mangling. Our mangle was always a vast disappointment to me. Compared with the massive cast-iron creations standing four feet high, equipped with great turning handles and massive button- crunching wooden rollers beloved of my grand mothers ours was a very modest affair. It had rubber coated rollers with a nice smooth action though of course muscle power was still needed to work it.

By this stage wicker clothes baskets were commuting twixt mangle and clothes lines strung between posts on the drying green. Clothes pegs of the day were hand-made wooden creations fashioned from hedgerow timber by the gypsies who hawked them round the district from time to time. Once pegged to the line washing was hoisted high on long wooden clothes props cut with a "V" at one end. No time was lost twixt pegging and hoisting for a large black and highly disreputable Labrador was kennelled on the drying green. You can take it from me he lost no time in marking his territory if washing hung too close to the ground! Given a good breeze and King Sol in his heaven the sheets, pants, knickers, shirts and Lord knows what else made a brave show as they billowed and flapped and dried..

Whilst Nature got on with the job outside the two ladies sat down to a well earned cup of tea and review of the latest gossip. After that Mother got on with housework and preparing dinner whilst Polly bucketed water to outside drains, washed and mopped the scullery floor and generally removed all traces of the morning's campaign.

Given a good drying day the next operation was ironing. I can just recollect those flat-irons being heated on a big coal-fired open range. They came in various shapes and sizes but Mother's fitted into a polished steel base with wire retaining clips which clamped it to the iron. Padded cloths were used to hold the handles and there was a constant toing and froing between range and ironing-board as they

cooled and needed replacing. I have often wondered whether that old refrain "Dashing away with a smoothing iron" had little to do with the actual ironing and everything to do with rushing back and forth with the irons.

Be that as it may there is no doubt that tea time came as a welcome finale to the days exertions. Given a good drying day piles of laundry stood neatly ironed and stacked ready for the airing cupboard and a general feeling of satisfaction pervaded the atmosphere. Tea finished Polly pinned her black hat in place, collected her black bag which would have mysteriously acquired a good filling of vegetables whilst Father was home for dinner and set out on her walk back to the village- come rain, hail or shine!

But what happened if sun and wind gave way to rain you ask? Good question. And the answer is simple. Wash day Monday became drying day Tuesday and ironing day Wednesday or - drying day Wednesday and ironing day Thursday! Just spare a thought next time you set the dial on the automatic washer!

9. The Foreigners Are In

Every Autumn the ranks of our native Shropshire woodpigeons were swelled by hordes of their migratory Northern cousins. Always referred to as "foreigners" their arrival was something of an event. At first there were a few scattered flocks and then overnight every wood and covert was full of them as they cleared acorns and beechmast.

A walk along a woodland ride sent flock after flock clattering from the trees ahead. Your progress was marked by a blue-grey wave constantly rising and pouring forward beyond the tree-top horizon. Were you to stand quietly and wait there they were again circling wide to right and left, coming in to alight behind and refill the vacuum created by your passage.

This welcoming feast of easy pickings lasted but a few days and then it was the open fields for them. Frosted potatoes, clover leys and stubbles in open weather, green crops as snow and frost gripped the land and for the remainder of the winter the woodlands served only as resting and roosting haunts.

Pigeons are voracious feeders and under certain conditions can play havoc with some farm crops. Every year two or three shoots were held to reduce their numbers as they returned to roosts across the Estate and neighbouring properties. Memories of many of these events still linger, odd incidents which stand out, but one occasion in particular I recall as clearly and vividly as if it happened yesterday. For one thing my father's brother, one Edward Ironsides, a somewhat larger than life character was staying with us at the time. We spent many the score of happy hours together.

They were roosting in their thousands and it was decided to organise a shoot on the next Saturday afternoon. Father got to work on the telephone and if everything went according to plan all the likely roosting places would be covered. Tenant farmers, beat keepers and a number of invited guns would all have taken part so that pigeons were kept well and truly on the move. That at least was the theory. In practice it seldom worked, for on the night someone, or two or three, the fellows who invariably complained most bitterly about damage to their crops, failed to turn up and that is where the pigeons pitched in for the night. On a windless evening it was that much easier for them to spot these gaps so we always hoped for a good stiff wind.

Though far too young to have begun shooting myself, I had spent many an hour sitting on a gamebag on the floor of a pigeon hide. For me, there was a fascination, not just in the sport itself, but in everything around and a trip to a great wood called The Terrace, particularly with that uncle was something of a highlight.

It is easy to see how many coppices and coverts came by their name but whoever called this majestic stretch of woodland The Terrace was most assuredly fired by a stroke of inspiration. All things natural are subject to constant change but at the time of which I write that mighty woodland was at the peak of its mature beauty. Its great oaks were interspersed with ash and elm, fine stands of beech, clumps and plantings of Scots pine and larch. Yew, holly, wild cherry and silver birch all found a home within its boundaries and, with a host of less abundant species, contributed to its natural splendour In Spring its floor was carpeted with acres of bluebells and snowdrops whilst great breaks of rhododendrons clothed huge sandstone outcrops which jutted and towered massively at intervals along its length. It was to one of these outcrops we were headed. It was known as Flag Rock and indeed the remains, some six feet or so of the old flag pole, were still embedded in it. For what purpose it was put there or when the flag had flown nobody could tell me but a pair of kestrels invariably nested on a convenient ledge and from the evidence on the old stump used it as a vantage point.

As a small boy I always felt slightly overawed on entering the wood. Its massive trees seemed ageless. It must, or so it seemed to me, have stood there since the dawn of time, must have watched the river forming itself in the valley gradually spreading out beneath our feet as we climbed, must have seen the first salmon run its course. Over the ages it must have given shelter to such a wealth of species, many long extinct, others confined to the wilder and more remote parts of these isles. Even so it was still a naturalist's paradise. Foxes, badgers, red squirrels, the advance guard of the grey invasion which sadly would oust the reds, but above all its teeming birdlife ranging from tiny goldcrest to soaring buzzard. All this added to excitement and anticipation as we arrived on top of the old rock and set about building a hide. A mighty strong gusting wind was blowing from a very chilly quarter and I was very glad of the shelter provided by the "rhodies".

Our hide was quickly built. First a few small branches were cut for the framework and then armfuls of dead bracken were collected to "brash" it in. On that exposed outcrop there was a break in the timber. A hide made all the difference for a pigeon has an uncanny, almost unbelievable ability for spotting an upturned face and swinging muzzle. A flick of tail and wings, a sideways jink and away he goes, accelerating, swinging and lifting a yard to the side of a perfectly well aimed charge. Not many have the ability to get in a second shot at such a target, still fewer are likely to make it tell. My companion of the day was one of that elite band.

Conditions were promising to say the least. A lowering sky and that stiff wind rising to nearly a gale at times were going to ensure our quarry left their feeding grounds in small irregular groups over a prolonged period. It also ensured their flying low over the tree tops, taking maximum advantage of every hollow and ridge to avoid the full might of that tearing wind. Most importantly, it resulted in the earlier arrivals flying for long enough over the swaying tree-tops before finally manoeuvring against the wind to a suitable perch.

Waiting could be frustrating but what compensations it held. Once the source of disturbance is removed it is surprising how quickly life in a woodland resumes its normal pace and tenor. From the slope below us came the rustling of dead leaves and bracken, then a pause followed by another rustle, a pattern oft repeated, sometimes louder, sometimes drowned by the wind, but unmistakably getting closer. Overhead a few small birds flew jerkily across our clearing and into the oaks behind. Their arrival was marked by urgent twittering, that hallmark of the tit population on the move. From branch to twig and twig to branch, their beaks in every cranny and crevice, their agility was a thing to marvel at. In twos, threes, fives and sixes, a continual stream poured across our patch of sky to swell numbers in treetops beyond. Already the leaders were passing beyond our horizon such was their energy and activity. One could but wonder at the wealth of insect life which must exist to support such a population. Great tits, blue-tits, long-tailed and coal, probably also willow but the latter often so difficult to distinguish from their cousins, all were there, mixing and intermingling.

This mingling of the species appears to be a characteristic of winter bird populations. Perhaps they complement each other in awareness of danger, their combined senses far outweighing that of an individual species. Whatever the reason there can be few more beautiful or fascinating sights then the tit tribes scouring winter tree tops in that final urgent burst of feeding activity before seeking their night's shelter from the elements

Apart from the tit tribe there were odd little flocks of finches, usually compact family gatherings of five or six, their dipping flight and whistling calls denoting bull finches or their green or gold cousins. Again there were the solitary denizens. Always a robin appears and a wren churred angrily not far away. One could only guess at the object of his wrath, maybe a weasel or perhaps a brown owl sitting tightly against the bole of a fir tree, motionless, imperturbable, head never moving but two amber eyes staring at you no matter how you circled his perch. His hour was yet to come. Tomorrow morning a puff or two of light brown feathers beneath a stand of young larches would probably mark the scene of his nocturnal activities. If so the noisy flocks of redwings and fieldfares beginning to criss-cross the sky would have provided his night's feast.

Uncle commented that it was time one or two were beginning to show up.There was my grandfather homeward bound from town already. From my lowly seat it was impossible to see the road but it was easy to imagine the scene. The old boy had still not succumbed to the advance of the motor car and preferred his horse and trap. He had a fine big cob, a chestnut called Bob who could fairly step out, and looking back they made a great sight rattling along. At that time of course it made little impression on me. It was merely another facet of everyday life and like my companion I was more concerned with the quest for pigeons.

Then suddenly-- there he was; beating slowly against the wind, a bulging crop all but hiding the head questing from side to side. A flexing of wings, that amazing acceleration and he was sliding away to join a bunch of woodies in a clump of beeches way above us at the top of the wood. Before he could land though they all rose with a clatter, steadied as the force of the elements met them and then beat away upwind. Someone had put them up and we speculated who it could be. Soon came noise of man and dog making a noisy descent through briars and undergrowth a hundred yards or so away. Loud and oft repeated yelling at the dog not only identified his owner but suggested a certain black labrador was having a rare old hunt. Soon the wild kek-kek, kek-upping of a rising cock pheasant and renewed urgency in appeals to the hound attested to the latter's success. He at any rate was having the whale of a time. Finally they both made it into one of the vast hollows a hundred yards away and the dog must have been tiring for peace descended again.

Not for long. That first solitary arrival which had flown away with the woodies had been the advance guard and small groups of pigeons were beginning to arrive over the wood. At first they passed too wide but finally I got the word to keep still and not look up. This lot would surely come in range. A slight movement, a readjustment as it were of the large brown Veldtschoens beside me and - bang. Tension was shattered loudly and abruptly. I listened for the tell-tale snap of a twig high above. None came and for a moment I thought he had missed. Then a rustle of rhododendron leaves and thump. We had opened the score. I was keen to dash off and collect the bird but was told to wait a moment or two. Others already perched in the vicinity would have been disturbed by the shot. Sure enough a bunch of twenty or so came back, wind in their tails, moving like an express train, and passed safely out of shot. How seldom a pigeon commits the error of flying over the gun which disturbed it. How many times since have I waited in expectation to be disappointed at the last moment, almost by the flick of a wing as it were.

With a final warning not to go too far downhill and fall over the edge of the rock I was on my way, emerging into a different world, a world where only the noise of wind in trees broke the silence. Gone now the tits and finches, our wren silent, all the to-ing and fro-ing and rustling of undergrowth at a standstill. Suddenly the skies were clear, no longer the highway of plover and starling, fieldfare and redwing. A lesser spotted woodpecker gave a solitary staccato call as his dipping flight carried him to a safer zone whilst jays shrieked far away in a stand of larch. As I rounded a rhodie bush, my footsteps crunching through the deep layer of dead bracken and leaves, a cock pheasant got up almost beneath my feet. Away he went, downdraught from his wings creating a distinct wake in the dead leaves. Even beneath that sullen sky his plumage captured enough light to burnish his bronze flanks. With red wattles and bottle green head shot with purple he looked magnificent as he racketed his way up and clear of the tree tops before setting his wings and accelerating away down the contour of the slope. Though quickly lost to view it was easy to visualise his rapid flight controlled only by the odd wing beat, his tail flickering in the wind as he dropped to the edge of the parkland below.

A few more paces and I spotted my pigeon a few yards from the base of the dead elm given me as a mark. Surely a foreigner and this one had a double handful of barley in his crop. Pointed ends of the grains could be felt quite easily through its thin skin. For a bird so often regarded as a pest to be controlled, the pigeon is a creature of great beauty. Few, if any, birds present such variation of colour to the observer. In spring sunshine those grey feathers can appear almost powder blue. On a winters afternoon over kale they are almost black whilst in differing lights that mauvish breast passes through all the shades from salmon pink to chestnut.

Soon there came the warning to freeze again. Once more the movement of feet, bracing of legs and a double shot followed by a single thud. I had spotted its final descent and was sent to collect. Judging by the lumps in the crop it had been feeding on beechmast. Was it, we wondered, one of our bunch from up the bank returning to try and fill an empty space or two before heading to roost?

As so often occurs, those first few shots were followed by a bit of a lull. Soon bird life began to be noticeable again and three carrion crows turned back by the first shot were going to have another go at crossing the valley. Their roost lay beyond the river and they had been working their way towards it. By no stretch of imagination could their progress be called a quiet one. Indeed if any bird gives continual notice of its presence it is a carrion crow. Those three rasping caws, constantly repeated give ample notice of their whereabouts yet of all the birds of the air few are better able to take care of themselves. Our trio were no exception. Unseen but heard repeatedly they would have been sitting hunched in those swaying beeches along the top of the wood. Now and again the odd exploratory sweep and circle out over the trees below but things would have to remain quiet for much longer before they made their run for home. Tonight they were going to have a long wait for pigeons were moving again. A couple of small flocks passed well out of range, their progress erratic on the buffeting wind.

Then part of a bunch settled out of shot. As so often happens a few which failed to make it first time swung round to try again giving the chance of a shot. On my way to collect this one a grey squirrel was legging it across the black network of branches, his grace and agility silhouetted against the greying sky. No doubt he had lain low perfectly concealed against a branch when first we appeared. Now his nerve had snapped and he was making all speed for a hole in a large tree. Now pigeons were coming in fast. No longer were they blue and grey but showing up darkly against the sky, small groups and larger flocks, all following the same course; arriving high from the fields they dropped rapidly to plough into that wind scything over the tree tops. Crops bulging, heads sweeping methodically from side to side they searched for a spot to pitch in, preferably to join earlier arrivals already ensconced in their roosts.

Suddenly it seemed the old wood was full of pigeons, Foreigners coming to roost in The Terrace in their thousands and shooting could be heard from all quarters. By any standards my uncle was a magnificent shot. Allied to great speed of reaction and co-ordination was a certain deadly application and on that winter's afternoon on Flag Rock he pulled out all the stops. Under any conditions pigeons coming to roost over high timber are never easy. They can present every kind of shot from the absolute sitter, to something as high and fast as driven game. Seldom do they give two similar shots running, nor are they like birds flying in the open where there is normally ample time to judge line of flight, speed and distance. With pigeons over timber much depends initially on spotting the bird, but probably the greatest skill lies in judgement of distance. It was here I always felt where E.I. had such an advantage. Time after time he pulled them from just inside extreme range. Only after I began shooting myself did full appreciation of that afternoon really develop.

Those odd bunches coming with the wind behind them were high and very, very fast. Once shot they pitched forward and downward in a wind driven ark which carried them over the ridge and down into the great hollow over which it towered. By no means did he hit them all but on several occasions took right and lefts out of them. Battling in against the wind they presented a completely different shot pitching and lifting, sometimes making headway, at others nearly stationary. At those the first barrel was relatively simple, but with the remainder putting on that amazing burst of jinking, lifting acceleration as they turned across wind, the second was an entirely different proposition.

Very often a pigeon killed stone dead, instead of crumpling and pitching earthwards.like most game, will set its wings and spin downwards for all the world like an ash key twirling. I know of no other bird which does this and the high proportion of pigeons which did so were always a feature of my uncle's shooting. In the conditions of that afternoon many of those birds were caught up by the wind and swept away from us. They too fell into the hollow beyond.

I mention this because an element of humour had crept into the proceedings. You may recall our friend with the labrador who had taken his stand some distance from us.Initially he joined in the general barrage firing one double shot after another at birds hopelessly out of range. After a while he stopped firing and it occurred to us that he had either given up or had moved further down the wood to try and find a better position. Not so. Whilst going to collect a pigeon from that side of the outcrop I found myself beaten to it by a portly black labrador. His tail-wagging progress took him back to a young fellow who was rapidly amassing a fairish bag. Somewhat indignant at this clandestine operation I conveyed the news back to the hide. E. I laughed out loud, commented that the young so and so should go far in life and no doubt his old man would be ringing my father later on to say how well his son and heir had acquitted himself.

When finally we finished the wind was waning as so often happens at dusk. Odd pigeons were still coming in, pitching purposefully downwards and clattering to rest wherever they could best make a landing. As darkness drew in they became increasingly less wary, almost reckless in fact, in their haste to secure the shelter of a tree top. By this stage many could have been shot sitting. Shooting was indeed still coming from many quarters but we had had enough. After the afternoon they had given us who could begrudge an easy passage for these latecomers. In any case it was time the old wood and its creatures were left in peace.

Of the thirty three pigeons I picked up that afternoon all but one were stone dead. For anybody used to shooting pigeons over high timber this alone tells the story. Many times since we have reminisced about that day and once, in an uncharacteristic moment of weakness the old boy went so far as to admit that though he might often have shot

as well, he never shot better. As we made our way downhill life around us was rapidly returning to normal. Pheasants were going up to roost, the hens almost noiseless, just a whirr of wings and occasional soft call, the cocks with their usual raucous clamour, a final defiant shout at departing day. Our grey squirrel had left his hole in the tree and was making for the greater comfort of his winter drey. Blackbirds were twink, twinking, as though mocking their pursuers of the day and high, very high above our black friends were thrice- cawing their way to roost beyond the river. Is it rejoicing at another day survived, a joyous release of tension as it were, or is it anxiety for the morrow? As E.I. so often remarked, there are really but two species in the wild ----The Quick— and The Dead!

My mother was a most wonderful cook and a superb meal invariably awaited our return from these expeditions. After this we all retired to enjoy a good fire in the sitting room where of course every last detail of the afternoon's events was relived. Sure enough the phone rang in the hallway and after a few minutes Father returned with a broad grin on his face. "That was the Count to say what a marvellous shoot his son had had. Twenty three pigeons and only twenty seven shots!

"Should make a grand shot", remarked E.I.

"Should make an even better politician" said Mother.

10. Two Trains

This is about two trains, memories of which, have remained with me throughout life.

In 1939 my mother took me to stay in Newcastle upon Tyne with that redoubtable soul Great Aunt Lizzie. Doubtless we were shown many a notable feature of her great city; alas, apart from the bridges over the Tyne and the shipping on it, I can recall but one; and that involved a railway train! It was called The Silver Jubilee and I was taken to Newcastle station to watch its departure for London.

All the carriages were indeed a brilliant silver whilst, to my great surprise, the engine was bright blue; and to even greater surprise was called The Golden----- Golden something? I forget. Now had it been The Silver something that would have made far more sense. Anyway it was one of those magnificent machines, the streamlined A4 Pacifics which held the world speed record and would itself doubtless notch a hundred as it sped Southwards.

We were watching a scene which somehow encapsulated the relationship between the great industrial hub which was Newcastle in those days and the nation's capital. It was a scene of bustle and affluence. Taxis bringing businessmen, all appropriately clad for their foray into centres of commerce, Whitehall ministries, and merchant banks. Chauffer driven limousines arrived with immaculately attired folk who strolled along the platform to their reserved compartments. In their wake came lesser cars with a cargo of ladies maids, valets and expensive luggage to be piled on trollies for porters to trundle towards the goods van; still more porters hurrying with hand luggage; the station master

himself in attendance to emphasise the importance of the occasion; the guard too of course, flag and pocket watch to hand; finally the man of the moment, the engine driver no less leaning benignly from his cab, king of all he surveyed, a thousand steam horses awaiting his bidding and from time to time disappearing from view as vast clouds of steam were vented and added to the general atmosphere of anticipation. Believe me we were not the only onlookers. There was a goodly crowd of people, all part of that whole scene of bustle and prosperity; mighty Tyneside of the 1930's.

Then came a great banging of carriage doors as porters worked along the train and, that job done, the guard seized the moment to blow his whistle and wave a green flag at the driver before disappearing smartly into his van. The driver too disappeared: then almost imperceptibly the train was moving, gliding slowly away. A gentle chuff or two and the pace increased. Then on went the power and by the time the last carriage cleared the end of the platform The Silver Jubilee was really moving.

Now to talk of another train and if memory serves correctly the year would have been 1943. A family friend used to visit Liverpool regularly on business; and on this particular occasion he took Mother and myself to see the great city. Whilst he attended to business matters before lunch we did some sightseeing and it has to be confessed I can recall precious little about it. Clearly recalled though was seeing my first black man and also a Chinaman; also my amazement at seeing them togged out, not in their national attire as always depicted in books of the day, but in the dull garb of your wartime British working man, even down to their flat caps. There was also that steam loco, a real railway engine no less, chugging quietly down the middle of a street, quite at home among cyclists, lorries and cars. A strange old world for a boy up from rural Shropshire!

After lunch our friend rejoined us and we went to see, indeed to ride on the celebrated Dockland Railway. That train ran the length of the docks, some five miles or so I was told. To board it we climbed a long flight of steps to a very elevated station platform. It would be totally impossible to imagine anything more different from the Silver Jubilee. Here was a work-a-day railway carrying work-a-day folk in a bomb scarred city, its passengers a mix of Royal Navy sailors, merchant seamen, dockers, port officials, workmen, stevedores, a mix which changed its blend at every frequent stop as some got off and others joined.

One side of the line was given over to quays, docks and dry docks,merchant ships, some being unloaded by cranes and stevedores into lorries and railway wagons which would pass beneath the elevated line to warehouses still standing intact among the bombed out shells around them. There were warships too, doubtless escorts for the merchantmen and like them painted in dull camouflage colours; all no doubt had run the gauntlet of the German U-boat packs in the Atlantic. Berthed in one dock was the battle cruiser Renown, sister ship to the Repulse which together with the battleship Prince of Wales was lost in the Pacific. At that tender age these grim facts did not occur, nor indeed were they pointed out to me. For a small boy there was just the thrill of riding on the overhead railway, of seeing the docks and shipping; of seeing that great strange world which was the mighty port of Liverpool.

11. Home Guard Heroics

When my generation finally drops off the perch so many good stories about the Home Guard will be lost. Every district has a wealth of them and here are some from the Norton and Beckbury area. The very fact the younger generation still laugh at Dad's Army suggests they are still worth recording.

Weekend training camps for the Home Guard were a feature of life in the early Forties and Apley Park was an ideal venue. It was the evening after conclusion of one of these camps when Kynaston Lloyd, the battalion bombing officer and Norman Sharpe his 2ic, were taking stock of things. The day's activities had produced three "duds" i.e. unexploded Mills hand-grenades. This was by no means uncommon as many of the grenades used in practice were of World War I vintage.

They assessed the situation. There were cattle in the Park and worse still there was nothing so certain as that kids would come and investigate the scene of the weekend activities. Left unexploded a guard would have to be posted and these fellows all had a job of work to go to next day. Trouble was Kynaston had only one demolition charge left. Tell you what : once everyone had departed they would collect and put the three together and hope one charge would do the trick

Bang went the charge and away sailed three duds to land, well scattered, one hundred and fifty yards away. By some happy chance Father had seen two drop and his companion the third one. So what now? Kynaston had a brainwave. They still had a sticky bomb left over from the day's activities. Now a sticky bomb was a device designed by an enthusiast for super enthusiasts to use. It was a short wooden handle with a metal sphere at one end. Press the correct button and metal casing flew off to reveal a sticky blob, inside which was a powerful lump of explosive all primed to go. They had been designed for use against soft skinned vehicles.

Fair enough then! Away went our pair of khaki geriatrics to collect the duds, the detonators of which, must surely have been getting mighty sensitive by this stage. Norman gathered his pair and later confessed he was more than careful not to shake them about too much. Friend Lloyd, as always, appeared completely unperturbed. There was a convenient dead tree trunk lying close by and beneath it a large burrow, clearly the work of a patriotic rabbit. They pushed the duds down the hole; then Kynaston activated the sticky fellow, shoved it on top of them and joined Norman behind a large beech tree. That did the trick alright; and branches came clattering down around them!

As ever the British army was advancing from the South along the Bridgnorth road. And as ever the orders were to harass and impede them whenever possible.Syd and Dick the two platoon signallers had been posted in the corner of one of the Leavenhalls fields where they had a good view along the road. A high hedge would have concealed their flag waving from the enemy whilst it could easily be seen from the command post on the rectory roof.

Time passed and our two sturdy lads felt the need for sustenance; so, very properly they set about the B and cheese whilst keeping an eye down the road. Not well enough though for the opposition spotted them first. A serious discussion on the finer points of gardening and beekeeping was rudely interrupted by the appearance of a couple of the enemy who had crept round behind them and pronounced them captured!

Were they worried? Not in the least. Dick took another bite before explaining to them that they had come from the wrong direction; so the best thing they could do was to bugger off and come back the way they were supposed to be coming!

Yet another invasion by the enemy hordes. At that time only the footpath separated South Lodge, the Agent's abode, from the main road. Father complete with hand grenades had positioned himself at a bedroom window overlooking the road. An exercise umpire, clearly aware of the defence plan, was not far away. They had not long to wait before a Humber scout car, a lightly armoured vehicle came slowly down the road. As it passed beneath the window the grenade was thrown. Bull's eye! Straight down the hatch and perhaps I should reveal now that the grenade was a paper bag filled with flour! A bag of flour you say? You have to be joking. But I certainly am not joking and I will bet a bob the crew of the Humber failed to see the funny side too.

Anyway the umpire stepped in and briskly ordered the vehicle out of sight. Soon a second Humber came rolling along. Repeat performance? Not quite. As the trusty throwing arm went back the paper bag burst. Exit one bomber leaving a trail of white footprints across the bedroom and down the back stairs. So are battles won and lost!

A bren gun carrier pulled up outside The Seven Stars in Beckbury. Out hopped the sergeant in command intent on giving his crew the opportunity to buy him a pint.

But a section of the local H G commanded by Frank Oakley were on the job and made short work of removing the distributor head. It was going to be good fun watching the ensuing pandemonium when the engine failed to start; then they would hand back the stolen part. Things do not always go to plan. An exercise umpire appeared on the scene and established not only the whereabouts of the crew but also the fact the carrier was immobilised. No use the local lads saying it was all a bit of fun. No sir! He reported in full.

It was the early hours of a wintry morning when the phone rang in our draughty old front hall. Father pattered downstairs in bare feet to stand on cold tiles and lift the receiver. It was Frank Oakley. "Norman" said he "do you know anything about courts marshals?" "Only that I wish the devil you were at one."

"Ah well", said Frank "that's just the trouble: I've got to go to one in Chester tomorrow."

Later Frank told father he had had a real old grilling during the proceedings. But what really upset him was the fact the poor old sarge caught it well and truly in the neck; needless to say the Beckbury lads felt really bad about it. "I'll tell you what" said Frank, "they can park the entire bloody tank corps in Beckbury from now on and we shall not be bothering it!"

12. Fortunes Of War

In the early years of the war a stick of bombs fell around home. One of them landed on the West bank but a few yards from the River Severn and about 150 yards upstream from the Wrens Nest. A bomb disposal squad from Cosford was soon on the scene and decided they had "an unexploded" on their hands. A demolition charge was prepared and the Kyte family and other locals in the immediate area were warned detonation would occur early the following afternoon.

It created a considerable explosion and immediately the Kyte family together with one or two others joined the demolition squad who were inspecting their handiwork. Incidentally Charlie Kyte was a life-long horseman and once told my father he had just ridden to his 80th Opening Meet of the Wheatland Hunt; his first was on a pony at five years of age! But I digress.

Mrs. Kyte had brought out tea and refreshments which were much enjoyed as they stood around chatting happily; doubtless with a considerable feeling of relief as they were assured by the squad commander that "there was no longer any danger and they could sleep soundly in their beds that night."

Refreshment and the day's excitement over they all made their leisurely way back downstream and had just reached the Wrens Nest when ---Up she went!! A huge crater was blown out of the river bank and remained an ugly reminder of a mighty fortunate escape for many years. Gradually though winter floods have healed that scar of war and restored the river bank to its original state.

13. Bagging The Brig

No fighting man likes being captured; least of all your fully made up, time serving Brigadier of the British army. Bad enough being put in the bag by some crack enemy unit in a foreign field, but to be taken prisoner by a pack of locals calling themselves Home Guard in the heart of rural Shropshire -------- now that was something else! Here is how it all came about.

In the aftermath of Dunkirk there was a year or two when the army seemed to be forever holding manoeuvres. All the local Home Guard units became involved and their orders never varied. " Harass and hold up the advance of the invading army by any means possible".

Now it so happened that the brigadier commanding this latest wave of invaders had chosen a secluded meadow beside the River Worfe in the parish of Beckbury as the perfect site to establish his command post. A narrow lane paused at a gateway before carrying on again as a farm track. Where this track ended was where the Brig had decided to contest ownership of the meadow with a herd of young cattle. Naturally they had taken the precaution of posting a sentry at the gate where the lane handed over to the cart track.

So far so good you might well think. You would be wrong because he had completely underestimated the capabilities of the local intelligence network: the Beckbury platoon of the Home Guard were only too well aware there was a big fish in their swim! How to catch him? Therein lay the problem.

Their solution, I think you will agree as you read on, was little short of brilliant. A member of the platoon, a gentleman called Rhodes,

owned a cattle lorry. He and another member with marked agricultural leanings donned their working togs. Then they officiated over the loading ramp at the rear of the vehicle whilst the uniformed snatch-squad climbed aboard. That done, up with the ramp, into the cab and away to go after their man.

Arriving at the lane end one of them leant out of the cab window and jovially accosted the sentry. " We've got a couple of young beasts we badly need to run with them others down here mate. Any chance of letting us through?"

Knowing a cattle truck and a local when he saw one, and clearly anxious to enter into the spirit of things the sentry cheerfully swung open the gate and waved them through. That part achieved the rest was all too easy. In no time at all the brigadier had joined the snatch- squad in the back of the lorry which was heading back along the cart track. Seeing the lorry coming back the sentry, helpful to the last, swung open the gate again and waved them on their way." Thank you me old mate!" " Any time pal!" You can imagine the scene, imagine too the look on the poor old brass hat's face as he listened to it all, surrounded by this pack of yokels, whilst standing in what cattle had left behind.

Perhaps not surprisingly he was beside himself with fury, absolutely fuming! In vain he protested the exercise could not proceed without him and would have to be halted. As one of the snatch party later remarked somewhat laconically, "By Gad the poor old lad was mad!" It was decided to keep him overnight at Harrington Farm where Frank Oakley lived, having agreed with an exercise umpire that they would release and return him at 9.00a.m. the next day.

By the time they got to Harrington Frank had just about had enough of his blustering. Passing through the rear quarters of the farmhouse they came to the cellar door. Frank stopped and opened it. " Now look here sir! It's like this. You can either spend the night down there---- or you can give your word of honour not to try and escape and have a bedroom instead." It was not a difficult choice, even for a brigadier, and later, over a cup of tea, the prisoner began to simmer down a little. " Tell you what sir " said Frank who could charm the birds off the trees, "I've got two or three farming pals coming in for a quiet drink this evening. How would you care to join us?"

Here at any rate, thought the brig, he would be on safe ground and lost no time in accepting. Had he ever seen the exploits of that little lot in the Commercial after an auction day he might not have been so keen! But how was he to know that and with a good fire up the chimney and the whisky flowing our seasoned campaigner set about showing these tit-pullers a thing or two about drinking. Was it midnight, or was it when the booze ran out? It hardly matters because whichever it was they still had to help him upstairs!

It had always been a point of honour with Frank that no matter how heavy the previous night's session he was always up and about next morning to meet his workforce on the dot. This attended to he went back indoors to rouse the prisoner for a bite of breakfast before returning him to active service.

But the prisoner was not in breakfasting form. Nor did he wish to be roused! No sir! He was nursing a hangover of monumental proportions and his bit of the war was going to have to wait a few more hours. Milk, aspirin, hair of the dog, black coffee, Andrew's liver salts, Frank knew the lot----and the lot were tried! Eventually they got him up and firing on enough cylinders to be sat in the farm van, the very one Frank used for collecting weaner pigs, and returned to the peace and quiet of that meadow beside the Worfe.

No! I'm sorry to admit local history does not record whether the same sentry was on the gate, or whether he, poor fellow, had already commenced a stint in the Glasshouse!

14. Christmas Cheer

Those years following World War II were mighty lean ones. Food was still rationed and anything in feathers was a rare luxury. Come Christmas it was an even greater luxury, and Christmas was fast approaching.

So that was the background against which this little story unfolds. Farmer Gordon had just finished killing his geese and there they were hanging by their feet all in a row. Friend Peter, a large and somewhat laconic character had called by to help, or perhaps to be more accurate, to watch whilst Gordon worked. At least it was someone to chat to.

Discussion of the latest goings-on was interrupted by a large car, a Humber Super Snipe no less, pulling up on the main road just outside Gordon's gate. These days it would be a nigh suicidal manoeuvre, but at that time it could well have been ten minutes before the next vehicle happened along.

They watched in fascination as a smartly attired gentleman got out of the car, crossed the road and came up the path to join Gordon, Peter and the geese in the outhouse. It transpired word had reached this gentleman that Gordon was perpetrating a slaughter of Christmas fare. Would it, he wondered, be possible to buy a goose?

A sale was quickly agreed and during the ensuing conversation the stranger remarked on what a long neck one of the geese had. At long last! It was the opportunity friend Peter had been awaiting. City type, big car, smart shoes, silk tie, smart suit -----now for a bit of fun.

"Ah well" said he breaking into the conversation," you see it's not really a goose. It's a swan!"

"Oh really" replied the stranger "how on earth did you come by that?"

"Oh it's no problem. They're always flying up and down the river here and we just give them one with the old twelve bore,"

The visitor was clearly taken aback. "But surely swans are a protected bird and killing them a serious offence?"

Peter blithely brushed this aside. Little things like that could never be taken too seriously, certainly not by lads like him.

"Well. Well. That is interesting. You see I happen to be the Chief Constable!"

Relating this tale later Gordon told me if ever you saw one fellow busy trying to convince another fellow that he had only been kidding; and it really was a goose with a long neck; and was not a swan after all --- Then that was our Peter!

15. By Dawn And Dusk

Every dog has his day; so too perhaps every fox. In our neck of the woods that must surely have been the years prior to 1914 when it was a toss-up which was more important on the estate--- good shooting or good hunting? Invariably it managed to produce both; but just how many who participated in either sport can ever have realised just how that was achieved.

It all began in the Spring of the year as a delicate green haze was claiming the woodlands, and foxes their territories. In the grey light of early dawn the staccato tapping of stone against stone could be heard as a line of keepers and their lads quietly moved Charlie towards a woodland ride or wood's edge where a second line waited, their hammer guns already fully cocked to avoid the metallic clicking caused by that action.

Perhaps the most surprising thing about a fox driven forward in this way was the amount of noise it made. Apart from the rustle created by its own movement there was always an ongoing progress report for those with the ability to read it. Jays, cock pheasants, magpies, chaffinches, blackbirds, wrens, hen pheasants taking wing; all contributed as though they knew what was afoot and were much in favour.

On these occasions some foxes came forward quite readily. Others though demonstrated an uncanny ability, that very hallmark of their kind, for locating the unmanned gap. Of course marksmanship was at a premium and good head gamekeepers could hide bad shots better than any cricket skipper ever hid a bad fielder. Even so mistakes did occur and the look of sheer disbelief as shot number one resounded from the wrong quarter invariably gave way to one of pained resignation as number two rang out, usually after an impossibly long pause.

This misfortune once befell an uncle of mine in the Via Gellia. He told how, drive over, he duly made his way uphill to peer over a dry stone wall and make his feelings known to the worst shot in Derbyshire. Peering over he was greeted by two very dead foxes, a look of sublime satisfaction and the more than apt comment, " Aye! An' that's bloody rattled thi!" It had too!

To return though to pre 1914 Shropshire. Those fox drives were executed quickly, efficiently and with the absolute minimum of noise. You must understand that to speak of killing, let alone be caught killing a fox, could result in someone looking for another job. Take it from me hunting was a serious business. So within an hour of daybreak fellows who had gathered from all over the estate were walking back to begin their day's work. The morrow's dawn would see them meet again, and again, until every wood and coppice, indeed every piece of cover capable of holding a fox had been covered

Of course a number of foxes always did survive these drives, and together with others which moved in across the boundary, provided a more than adequate breeding stock. There were few beats without an active earth or two so there was still plenty left to do. Only a beat keeper who has experienced the damage foxes can cause could fully appreciate just how vital it was.

Nesting populations were where the real damage was done. By no means every fox developed this ability for taking nesting birds, but when it did occur, results could be devastating. To this day I vividly recollect the commotion created by one particular fox taking twenty six partridges from known nests on one beat in less than a week. And just how many unknown one wonders? The culprit was quickly located and there was no further trouble.

Charlie's bird-nesting was not without its element of humour. Every keeper had his "fail-me-never" for protecting nesting birds. Devices ranged from the mystical bunch of herbs to the downright filthy use of a liquid aptly named "Stinks". Despite the extravagant claims on their behalf they all proved largely useless. Early in the '20's the ultimate in anti-fox devices made its appearance. Some bright lad sold the idea of hanging a luminous disc a couple of feet or so above the nest. Swaying and twisting in the wind they produced an eerie phosphorescence

which was visible for scores of yards on a dark night. Father was one of a great many who must have tried these discs. Initially they were an unqualified success, but as so often occurs when man tempts nature, retribution was waiting in the wings. It was soon realised the odd canny fox was associating discs with food and was losing no time in taking advantage of this thoughtful act on the part of the old foe!

So back to the earths and the fellows who had game to rear. Something had to give so once again poor old Charlie caught it in the neck. Dusk was the crucial time for that was when the dog roused himself to go to the earth and join the vixen as she left. This was an opportunity, and it was usually the only one, to get a shot at him. Now your wild dog-fox can look after himself rather better than most in the animal kingdom. Slightest miscalculation with wind, noise or concealment was fatal, and the degree of skill, patience, not to mention sheer low cunning involved was neither quickly nor easily acquired. On one occasion my father saw the dog approaching, but he obviously sensed trouble and circled out of range repeatedly screeching like a vixen, a clear warning to his mate in the earth. No mistake about the sex. It was definitely himself!

With the dog accounted for the vixen could be dealt with. When leaving an earth they lose no time about it. This fact, perhaps more than anything else, has contributed to the myth that foxes always travel a distance to hunt. Usually though they quickly leave the immediate vicinity and whilst in Essex my grandfather knew of an earth flanked by a sitting hen pheasant one side and a tenanted hare sett on the other.

Getting a shot at a vixen leaving at dusk was never easy. One moment nothing; the next a fleeting target with an uncanny ability for finding and using dead ground. Then again it was by no means unusual for them to simply stay in late on these occasions! Other times they forgot the rule book and left long before dusk. One such vixen once gave Father an almighty shock. He had selected a sandy knoll which afforded an ideal vantage point. He waited, and he waited. He waited in fact until it was clear nothing was going to happen that evening. Just as he was about to get up and depart, doubtless with his thoughts turning to other matters, she gave that unearthly vixen's screech within feet of his ear! No, he did not go back the following evening for he knew that come next sunrise those cubs would be in a new abode anything up to a quarter of a mile distant. It was a case of-----start looking again!

With dog and vixen accounted for it was a simple matter to clear up the cubs. If young, and provided the earth was away from the beaten track, they were easily trapped. As often as not though they were dug out. At the culmination of such a dig one of the keepers seized a hissing snarling little ball of fury, and holding him eyeball to eyeball, was explaining that pheasant would never be for him. Much to the hilarity of his companions the cub somehow managed to make a dive and get him by the nose. The resultant deep scars were a source of acute embarrassment to the nose's owner for many a long day. I have only known one other fellow bitten by a fox --- but that is another story!

Of course not all cubs were killed. On most beats an older litter was spared and their upbringing taken over by the old foe. If the good Lord imbued dumb animals with a sense of humour then those cubs must have indulged it to the full. To suddenly find themselves in comfortable strawed accommodation, thrown the daily rabbit or hare, or joints from fallen livestock by way of a change, to be cleaned out regularly by the keeper's lad, even indeed the keeper himself on occasion, now that must surely have given them supreme satisfaction!

As soon as possible they were returned to the wild where hand feeding continued until it was certain they were fending for themselves. By the time they heard horn and hound they were wild animals with all the guile and cunning of their kind. In short they were mighty well equipped to take care of themselves.

16. Great Expectations

One day in the late nineteen twenties they were fox hunting in the Spring Coppice. Charlie had broken, and as invariably happened, had taken a line straight for a magnificent strip of woodland, a mighty safe haven, known as The Terrace. Pack and field were away in hot pursuit across the Home Farm fields.

Suddenly a solitary rider who had been left stranded at the far end of the copse appeared on the ride leading to a field gateway. One of the many lads who were apt to award themselves a day off school on these occasions spotted him and dashed to open the gate. Standing not far away, leaning on his stick in characteristic pose, whilst keeping a fatherly eye on proceedings, was one Jimmy Reece. A great and much beloved character, Jimmy was an elder statesman amongst the game-keeping fraternity.

As the lad swung the gate wide open the rider came cantering through. Then, making the divots fairly fly as he urged his mount to a gallop across the turf, he yelled back over his shoulder. "Give the boy sixpence Reece --- I'll pay you back later!"

Jimmy eyed the lad. And the lad eyed Jimmy!

"Boy", said Jimmy "you heard what the gentleman said?"

"Arr, I did an' all Mr Reece!" replied the lad, his face a study in expectation. Sixpence was a very tidy sum at that time and would have made mighty serious inroads into the colourful line of sweet jars adorning the top shelf of Harry Thomas' village shop.

"Well boy," said Jimmy not unkindly "When I collect my tanner --- that is when you'll get yours!"

GIVE THE BOY SIXPENCE

It is just possible that in this year of our Lord, nineteen eighty eight, the lad is still waiting. Jimmy gave up many the long year since.

17. Fire Fire

Farm fires, particularly where livestock are involved, have always been one of farming's worst nightmares. This was a bad one and if memory serves correctly the year was 1928. That night something awakened my father who was sleeping in a house a good quarter mile distant. Immediately aware of an unusual light in the bedroom he hopped out of bed and across to the window. And there it was --- the Home Farm going up like the proverbial torch.

Telephoning failed to arouse John Davis the farm bailiff of the day, so it was on with a few clothes and down to the farm house where he finally succeeded in bringing that gentleman to an upstairs window. Flinging it open poor old John could only manage to exclaim "No it can't be!" But alas it was. Harvest had but recently finished and fire was spreading through eighteen bays of Dutch Barn and also adjacent stacks in the yard.

Before leaving home Father had also alerted the Apley fire brigade which was based at the Hall for in a remarkably short time that horse drawn outfit arrived at the gallop. A driver, four men to man the pump and run out hosepipe all under the command of Jack Weston the Hall electrician.

Now in the poultry yard there was a circular brick lined duck pond built not only for the pleasure of ducks but also to act as a water supply in the event of a fire. Running out of hose from pond to pump, and pump to fire, was completed with commendable efficiency and frantic pumping began. Their combined exertions produced fountains of water the length of the hose but devil a drop from the nozzle! During my brief sojourn in the British army I once witnessed the identical performance. It was a fire drill and if nothing else the sight of the barrack square being irrigated from end to end produced mighty cheering from the assembled ranks.

I bet there was not much hilarity at the Home Farm that night though and it would have been no small relief when the Bridgnorth brigade eventually arrived. Not that there was anything they could do for the barns and stacks: it was a question of saving the buildings by spraying with water. After three days they rated it safe to leave. Since they had emptied, not only the duck pond but also a two acre sheet of water known as the Long Pool, it was clearly the correct decision. So there we are. Best part of a hundred years ago and lost in the mists, or should it be the smoke, of time.

What started it would have been the question of the day? No one knows. What is certain though is that in those days the Home Farm always employed a youth from a city orphanage. These lads lived with a local family, worked on the farm, and the poultry yard being their prime responsibility, were always known as the cock boy. The current holder of the title was a prime suspect but after thorough investigation was eliminated. However, after he left a number of fires marked his progress around the country and he was eventually caught and convicted as an arsonist. Was he indeed the culprit? Who can tell?

Every night until his final retirement in 1948 John Davis, my grandfather incidentally, lit a hurricane lantern at 10p.m. and did a final round of stack yard and buildings. No way was he so foolish as to think that in itself would prevent another arson attack; but I do know for certain that the memory of seeing an excellent harvest, a whole year's work, go up in flames, always weighed mighty heavily on him.

18. Blast Him

It surely caused a stir locally. Word had somehow got around that a guest of the Major called Droga Montague was going to arrive piloting his own aircraft. Touchdown was to be late in the afternoon of an autumn day, the chosen landing ground being a thirty acre grass meadow close to the Home Farm. One end was bounded by a lane rejoicing in the name Cheswardine; and that was where the reception party, together with a good old crowd of locals had assembled. Another small gathering, of which I was one, waited at the other end of the field on a farm track known as the Sock Pit Lane.

My grandfather, the Home Farm bailiff of the day, had organised a good old bonfire at the Cheswardine end together with a heap of wet hay. Once the plane was spotted the wet stuff would be heaped on the fire to produce copious smoke - the next best thing in the absence of a wind sock.

We waited patiently at first, and then impatiently, until at long last there was the sound of a low-flying aircraft. Suddenly, quite amazingly huge and noisy, it was but a few feet above us. Aeroplanes had always been those little things in the sky and to see and hear one so close was something of a shock. I can see it now, a blue and silver monoplane descending rapidly. Soon it touched down. All very impressive. Only one slight snag - the field proved to be not quite long enough! Doubtless the Major had anticipated welcoming his guest at the field gate. He need not have bothered for having crashed through the far hedge the pilot was able to step down onto the lane itself.

As for Grandad: well he was furious. That hedge had been planted but a few years earlier and was about ready for laying. Planes could soon be repaired but hedges take years to grow; and here was this damn fool making a blasted great gap in it. Blast him! And blast his aeroplane as well! Blast you see was the one word Grandad invariably resorted to when others failed him. Indeed in some less respectful quarters he was known as Blastit Davis!

19. Cometh Wheels - Cometh Fergies

It is always tempting to think of "The War Years" as that time when mechanisation swept through farming and changed it for ever. Should you ever have watched archive film of "War on the Land" you may be forgiven for thinking the countryside teemed with Catterpillar crawlers and lines of Fordson tractors nonchalantly driven by landgirls both buxom and carefree!

Perhaps it really was like that in some parts. In our neck of the woods though mechanisation barely succeeded in bridging the gap between vastly overstretched workforces and the ever- increasing demand for production. It was not so much the scale of change which was amazing --- it was the nature of it. Those years gave birth to the developments to which so much present day farm machinery owes its existence. At that time of course we were not sated by innovation and anything new really was a source of intense local interest; often indeed of real excitement.

My great stamping ground was the Home Farm which by the standards of the day was a very large and well farmed mixed enterprise. My recollections of the war years on that farm are surprisingly vivid so I will restrict myself to describing the innovations which happened there.

So what are my first recollections of mechanisation? Believe me or not --- it was wheels! It would have been 1939 and Grandfather Davis took me to look at three new muck-carts he had seen and bought at an agricultural show. I have a strong feeling it could well have been the last Royal prior to the war. Anyway there they were, resplendent in red and

green. But it was not the paint he wanted me to look at. No sir --- it was the wheels! Unlike those huge, traditional iron-rimmed timber creations which sank deep into soft going these jobs were metal: half the diameter, but with big fat pneumatic rubber tyres. They would ride on top of soft ground and be so much easier for the horses. That was what really enthused him --- they would be that much easier for the horses!

And it was not only the horses which were to benefit from this pneumatic marvel. There was the guy who wheeled the sacks of grain on a threshing day. A new sack barrow with pneumatic wheels brought a whole new dimension to his task. This may sound all too trivial, but you try pushing a two hundredweight sack of corn across a bumpy yard on a pair of cast iron wheels!

Shortly after the muck-carts another set of pneumatic wheels arrived but this time fitted to a tractor. A second Case had been bought to double the Home Farm tractor fleet. Used as we were to seeing tractors bobbling or should I say hobbling around on iron wheels, this was another astounding innovation. Only one question remained and that an important one. Would the rubbers grip as well as the old flat wheels with their triangular studs or lugs? No need to have worried. They gripped all right, probably better in fact. Tractor designers had long struggled to break out of the old traction engine mould and this innovation was a big stride down that road.

Another early memory was a new elevator. I can well recall its predecessor. Who could ever forget it, for it was horse, or rather pony powered. Round and round, hour after hour, harnessed to the end of a pole, which ended in a cogwheel, which drove a shaft ending in another cogwheel --- which turned the elevator! So long as the old pony plodded the endless circle, corn sheaves trundled up the elevator and on to the stack. Sometimes the old boy stopped plodding; then following vocal encouragement from both stack and waggon - off he went again. You can imagine the scene.

With the arrival of this new machine the pony was pensioned off to end his days as companion and mentor to the last two Shire colts ever to come onto the farm. He promptly registered his appreciation by leading his two protégés on a raid into our veg garden where they decimated the winter greens. But it all proved too much for the old lad for he was found dead next day, presumably from a surfeit of cabbage! He really was an old boy too, for the best local estimates placed him nearer forty than thirty.

This new elevator was a really smart affair by Bamford, or was it Blackstone? Anyway it began with a "B" and had a removable set of tubular steel shafts to enable a horse to move it. More to the point though it had its own little engine. A pound to a penny this would have been a Lister or a Petter two-stroke. Ten pounds to a halfpenny it would have been a pig to start from cold and an absolute swine when hot!

Invariably these little beasts developed a rapport with someone, usually a motor cycle enthusiast possessed of the mechanical wizardry and charm to coax them back to life. Beasts or not they were marvellous once started. Here at last was a source of lightweight, portable power which over the next few years would transform many a slogging chore.

For instance it was not long before a new potato riddle or grader joined the strength and this again was driven by one of these little motors. Gone were the days of hand riddling as Mr. Edlington's machine gently rocked away at the end of the clamp. An ingenious combination of riddles and chutes removed the smaller tatties before sending the remainder up and over a rolling belt. Any rejects could then be removed by hand, leaving the bulk to fall over the end to be swallowed up by a hundred-weight hessian sack.

It would have been shortly after the elevator had its face-lift that another kind of motor appeared on the scene. During the early war years those magnificent granaries were requisitioned for storage of flour away from the risk of bombing. It would have been the Ministry who installed the hoists for loading and unloading flour lorries. These were powered by electricity and remained for use by the farm after the Ministry left. The electric motor had arrived! Today they provide power for a vast range of farming activities. Come to think about it many farms were still without electricity in those days!

A year or so later the potato field was again the setting for another great leap forward. The limiting factor for any machine drawn by horses, or indeed tractors, had always been the ability of the wheels to transmit sufficient power to the working parts. It would have been about 1944 when the Oliver potato digger arrived on the scene. Simple enough in concept it had a steel blade to lift soil and tatties onto a rotating elevator chain constructed of bars linked at their ends. This in itself was quite a breakthrough as it allowed soil to fall away before depositing a lovely compact swathe of tatties over the back. No way could the wheels have generated and transmitted this amount of power. Instead it came from the tractor engine via a rotating steel shaft rendered flexible by a "Universal" coupling, in itself a considerable breakthrough, which was attached to a power take-off point at the rear of the vehicle. For the first time we had a machine both powered and towed by a tractor.

Quite early in the war, '42 or '43 for a guess, we all got terribly excited by the arrival of a crawler tractor. This really was progress! Admittedly it was only a small crawler, and if memory serves correctly, ran on tracks no wider then 5 or 6 inches. It was called a Cleetrac and had it proved mechanically reliable would have been invaluable. Sadly that was not the case. According to Grandfather the tracks were its weakness: this was in total contrast to those of the caterpillar crawlers used in the forestry which were the ultimate in reliability.

How it came to be on the farm is a bit of a mystery. Its khaki livery suggested it was part of some Ministry scheme to boost productivity. Doubtless the makers of the little tractor would have been delighted to welcome the men in bowlers! Certainly my grandfather never bought it and was soon blessing, or more probably blasting, the time being wasted on keeping it going. Suffice to say its sojourn was brief!

A completely different story can be told about the next tractor to arrive at the home Farm. Seeing it for the first time anyone could have been forgiven for wondering if it really was a tractor. If so, would it actually pull anything? Earlier we mentioned the obvious influence of traction engines on tractor design. This new arrival, the Ford Fergusson, not only cracked the mould --- it shattered it! With a speed of 15 m.p.h. at that time a veritable racer, it was small, compact, quiet and wonderfully easy to steer. It sported not only a self-starter operated via the gear stick, a most wonderful safety feature, but the option of individual brakes on the rear wheels. Even more amazingly it boasted a power take-off point and hydraulics! Hydraulics, let us say the word again, had arrived on the farm! Hydraulics operated the three-point linkage system still used today which enables implements to be attached to and lifted by the tractor. Joined like this tractor and implement become one machine where for example, a plough is worked, it automatically transfers extra pressure to the rear driving wheels creating better traction.

You may rest assured there was no shortage of sceptics when that little tractor arrived. Wise shaking of heads, knowing looks and "What in the name of hell did the gaffer think he was playing at?!" Once put to work the new grey tractor soon confounded the prophets of doom with its work-rate and versatility. "You'd wonder how the little bugger does it," was now heard from many quarters. Praise indeed! But even that paled before the final accolade. That happened when the Ford Fergusson became ….. "The Fergie!"

Grandfather would certainly have done his home-work before buying The Fergie. He did confess though, "strictly between the two of us you understand," that he never really expected its performance to live up to the claims made for it. What had really swayed him was its road speed. With some fields lying more than a mile from the buildings transport was a major headache. If only it would help crack that problem anything else was a bonus. Cracking one problem immediately created another. Now it was a case of finding a trailer to match the tractor! Grandfather's solution, at least in the context of the day, was nothing short of brilliant. Off he went to a local blacksmith. Like so many of his calling Sammy was moving with the times. Welding was another quantum leap in the field of agricultural machinery and this guy could do it.

Sammy was given a plan sketched in pencil on the back of a used envelope (paper was scarce in wartime). From it emerged three new trailers, dillies we called them, plus a couple of pairs of shafts mounted on axles with pneumatic wheels. Like the Fergie these trailers completely shattered the mould of traditional design. Low to the ground, loading made simple by high ripples at each end, they had a welded steel chassis, a single axle with pneumatic wheels, and a tractor mounting hitch or clevis. They carried more than the old four-wheeled wooden wagons and when empty were light enough to be manoeuvred by one strong man --- or two lesser mortals!

In their own simple way the dillies were another giant stride. Horse and shafts were used to pull them whilst loading in the cornfield. For the journey home they were hitched to the Fergie. The day of those great wooden four-wheelers lurching, crunching and jolting into the stockyard behind a pair of sweating shires was but another memory!

One advance invariably leads to another and a couple of years after the dillies appeared a new device arrived in the hayfield. Best described as a mobile elevator it was towed by a tractor. Hay was lifted from the swathe and conveyed aloft by kickers similar to those in a threshing box. A dilly was hitched in tandem behind – or was it in front (I really forget). Anyway, thanks to those high ripples on the dilly a single loader could cope, though I suspect there could be heated exchanges between him and the tractor driver! This machine reigned but briefly, for it was destined to be replaced by the tractor – mounted haysweep, an invention of elegant simplicity. For a brief year or so the principle reappeared in the guise of "Cut-lifts" used for silage making, only to be superseded once more by the Buck-rake and Cutter-blower. Fleeting or otherwise its brief sojourn marked the end of the hand pitching of hay! Interesting to reflect also that this was the only one of the innovations to hit the Home Farm which cannot still be seen in use today.

Now was it '44 or'45? I really can not remember. Of one thing though there is absolutely no doubt --- its arrival caused an almighty stir in the neighbourhood! A Combine! An Oliver combine no less, resplendent in aluminium paint and boasting a seven foot cutter-bar and sails. Towed by a tractor it was powered by its own motor and had a platform where a fellow stood to bag off the grain. Once full jute sacks were slid down a shute with a retaining gate at the bottom and only when three bags were in the shute was the gate tripped to slide them out onto the ground to await collection. Compared with the self-propelled monsters of today it was a toy, but at the time it was yet another giant stride into the future! A machine which not only cut the grain but threshed and bagged it as well.

Of course we lads had heard all about combines and not surprisingly I had quizzed dear old Grandfather on the matter, doubtless in a way which implied it was about time he got abreast of things. Very patiently, but in a manner which put one smart young pup very firmly in his place, he had explained why combines were not really suited to our way of farming. At best they could only be a short-term expedient, because unlike the system in use, most of the rubbish – by which of course he meant weed seed, fell back on the land.

So here he was with the first combine to arrive in the district! What had happened to make him change his mind? What had become of the oft-quoted and much revered principle of "always letting some other clown be the first to try out new ideas? - Always keeping a close eye on how they worked on course!"

Once more the patience showed for he was the most kindly of men. His words must have made a great impression for they are still fresh in my memory. "You see," he began "with any luck this war is not going to last a lot longer: but my old work force is getting very, very tired. Hopefully this contraption will help see them through to the end. If it only achieves that much it will have served its purpose". How was he to know that selective weed-killers were just beyond the horizon and would appear in time to secure a lasting role for the combine --- that it would come to symbolise the ultimate, the very pinnacle of progress in power farming!

20. The Thousand Pound Pig

It will hardly seem possible to you youngsters but there have been occasions when people in this country have been mighty hungry. Nobody actually starved during World War II, or the lean years which followed, but preoccupation with food, or rather the shortage of it assumed major proportions. If someone began by saying "Do you remember …" it was a dead cert we were about to be treated to some gastronomic anecdote of pre-war vintage. It was equally certain that the aspiring raconteur would get short shrift, "Shut up! You're making us hungry."

Now it was during one of those hungry years when a certain farmer killed the pig in question. Truth to tell that particular farmer quite often killed a pig together with other creatures great and small. Like everyone else he required a licence to kill a pig and that licence only permitted the killing of one pig – per annum!

Flouting the law to this extent was not without its hazards. It only required the slightest slip to ensure star billing in the local rag. "Well Known Local Farmer Faces Black Market Charge". Well known now if never before that is. Of course risks could always be minimised by a little sensible insurance.

Take the local bobby. How could he deny his family the chance of a good tuck-in; provided of course it came off the regulation pig? And the man from the Ministry too. A warm heart and a hungry little tummy lurked behind that bleak exterior. So what if the annual pig did die quarterly or even monthly? Tragic little mistakes did occur, always the odd rotten apple, but on the whole the system worked smoothly enough. Seldom did the local media roll out those dreaded headlines.

Anyway back to the story of our farmer and his pig. By today's standards it was a good big pig, not huge but certainly substantial. A friend of mine was great mates with the teenaged son of the house and these two lads invariably helped with the illicit killing and cutting up. This earned a few bob. Rabbits caught during the week earned a few more so that most Saturday evenings they were able to join the majority of country folk in whooping it up a little.

One frosty evening several weeks after the pig in question had been killed my friend called round to collect his mate. As usual he went in the "back way" through an unlit scullery, its collection of boots, buckets, egg boxes and Lord knows what peeping from the shadows, and on into the kitchen. Farmhouse kitchens have always fascinated me; my friend too apparently for he described this one almost lovingly. He enthused over the flickering range, black leaded, burnished and flanked by copper warming pan and wooden fire bellows. He waxed eloquent about the brass oil lamp and the mellow light it shed. And the table itself, scrubbed as in those days they were, and scrubbed again until it was quite impossibly white. But most of all his memory dwelt fondly on a huge ham, lying in state as it were, on that very table. Even his impressive descriptive powers were stretched to the limit doing justice to that ham.

Our farmer came in and told the pair of them to "'ang around a while" as he was expecting a customer for the ham; a bookmaker from Doncaster no less. Sure enough there was soon the sound of a car drawing up in the yard. Peeping out they could see it was a great big opulent car and climbing out it was its owner. As his feet sounded outside the two lads were told to make themselves scarce. So, they retreated to the darkened scullery taking mighty good care to leave the door sufficiently ajar to keep an eye on proceedings. Neither of them had ever seen a bookie before and this was too good a chance to miss. Nor were they disappointed. Large and opulent though it was, the car had nothing on its boss. A great big florid fellow sporting a showy cravat, an equally loud check suit, mustard waistcoat, everything you could wish from a member of his calling. Nor did he speak in a whisper!

"By gum! But that's some ham!" All this with the air of a man who appreciated the good things in life. "Well", said our farmer, "it's just fifty punds". Clearly he was preparing the ground for a good haggle and was

about to explain, "that at sor much a pund that would amant to ...." But hold it! A large fat hand with a huge gold ring was already making for an inside pocket. Better still it re-appeared with an even fatter and larger wallet. This was opened with that certain flourish, the very hallmark of all good bookies. One by one ten magnificent white fivers were counted out and laid imperiously beside the ham.

Our lads faces must have been a picture. Our farmers certainly was as he suddenly found his voice and yelled for someone to "Come and give an 'and carryin". There was more than a hint of ceremony as the great ham was borne out of the kitchen, down into the yard and finally laid reverently to rest in the boot of the car. There it was made comfortable beneath a variety of rugs, overcoats, binoculars, shooting sticks, luncheon baskets and what have you (after all one couldn't be too careful in those days). Finally the boot was closed, the bookie manoeuvred behind the great wheel as happy as one of his punters who had just notched a forty-to-oner, and the great car and ham headed into the night and for Doncaster. For a few moments no one spoke. There was no shortage of puddles along the lane and the noise of the car crunching the ice on them carried a surprising distance.

Suddenly our farmer broke the silence. "Well lads, I reckon one o' them fivers belongs to you!" Were they hearing things? Sensing an air of incredulity, if not downright disbelief he carried on. "Aye. I reckon you've earnt it fair 'an square!" By gum, it was true. Never did the old lamp cast light on three happier faces than came back to the kitchen to share the spoils.

After my friend had recalled the story the other evening we indulged ourselves in the harmless if somewhat futile pastime of comparing prices then ad now. We reckoned that even at the price originally intended, that old pig would have been a Thousand Pound Pig in today's currency. A thousand pound pig and yet today he would still leave the farm gate at a tenth of that. Across the counter of course he would be rather more, say two and half times more.

But this was never meant to be a homily on who, if anybody makes the money out of pigs. I rather hope another message, the real message, might shine through the humour. My friend summed it up rather nicely. "Y'know, I reckon that owd bookie must 'ave bin fair longin' for a bite o deacent meeat."

21. Sunday Mornings

What better way for a lad to spend a Sunday morning than roaming a farm with his grandfather? You see at that time there was a war on and there were precious few Sundays when my father was not away on Home Guard duties. So down the road it was to where the grandfather in question was bailiff, or in modern parlance, farm manager of the Home Farm on a large Shropshire estate.

Now this was no ordinary farm. It could only have been designed as a model farm and as with Old MacDonald's it had to have something of everything. Unlike Old Mac's, I suspect, it had a most magnificent range of buildings built during the 1800's. Rest assured no expense had been spared. It would be amazing if some clown has not listed them by now

Take the poultry yard for instance; two sides of it were bounded by brick, yes I repeat brick built, housing for turkeys, ducks, fattening cockerels and laying hens. No geese or guinea fowl in my day but I bet they featured in the original plans. A circular brick lined pond catered not only for the ducks but acted as the water supply in the event of fire. Had it not been for one of the estate painters working up a ladder and spotting me taking an unscheduled bathe in it I would not be writing this now. But back to the farm. There was even a pigeon loft topped by an imposing tower and weather vane. The farm office was fronted by a weighbridge which I can only ever recall being used to weigh the bull, which to the delight of all concerned, topped the ton.

Back to the poultry yard. Its produce had to be plucked, dressed, date-stamped and despatched for use by the Hall. A small herd of

Dairy Shorthorns, Channel Islanders and Red Polls were hand milked to provide milk, butter, cream, buttermilk and skimmed, again for the Hall. In addition farm staff and one or two other families received free milk. Twenty four pounds of butter were made twice weekly. During the early war years, with labour at a premium, I recall my mother relieving my grandmother of the job, for hand churning that quantity of butter can be surprisingly hard work.

Surplus skimmed went to the pigs mention of which immediately evokes memories of the old swill tub. A great wooden barrel mounted on a pair of steel rimmed wooden wheels, it could be hitched behind a pony and float. There were two of them and whilst one was being filled with kitchen waste at the Hall the other stood outside the piggery where its contents, together with any other edible farm waste such as reject tatties were boiled up for the inmates. Waste was never an option in those days.

It always made my morning, when having harnessed and hitched up the nag, we set off down the park with the empty tub trundling and rumbling along behind. Truth to tell I believe the old boy seized any possible opportunity to feel a set of reins in his hands. On one never to be forgotten occasion he handed them to me. "Go on. You drive him." Imagine the thrill. Imagine too the panic when the entrance to the hall yard hove into view! Nearer we got the narrower it looked. "Just point him at the middle and you'll be alright" came the voice from above. Phew! We made it and rattled to a halt on the cobbles.

Whereupon, as though in celebration, the nag lifted his tail and deposited a neat little pile. He was instantly adjudged a bugger—and a rather dirty one at that. In the same instant my mother's earnest exhortations to try and be like my grandfather and never to swear also bit the dust." Blast him! A whole blasted mile to do it and he has to do it here. He never fails. Blast him." Incidentally blast was a favourite word of the old boy When working with the shepherd that old nag responded to the call of nature with gay abandon wherever he happened to be, but take him into that Hall yard --- Ah well. Ponies are noted jokers and he was one of the best. Not surprisingly his antics were well known and catered for by the Hall staff who always left a broom and shovel for use by the swill team.

Earlier I mentioned no expense had been spared and as though to prove the point that farm boasted a full blown factory chimney. Apart from providing a vantage point for the farm pigeons it served a steam

engine which powered a whole range of machinery; belt driven root cleaners and slicers, chaff cutters, oilseed crushers and doubtless others. Originally I can only think its main function would have been to drive a threshing box.

When last I kept sheep the value of the fleece barely covered the cost of shearing. It had also become standard practice to roll the fleece loosely How things change. On the Home Farm the wool clip was to be seen in beautiful neat tight rolls each secured with a twisted rope of fleece and stored in one of the granaries. Before clipping those sheep would have had a good old swim in a clean pond, for in those days it was always reckoned the wool-clip paid the shepherd's wages.

Things do indeed change!

Of course the Herefords, together with the horses, were my grandfather's great love. There were few Sunday mornings he failed to slide open the feeding hatches of the bull pens and gaze fondly at the occupants. Great placid looking beasts; but be not deceived. Once I saw one of them clear a five barred gate from a standing start. Another time I sped past William on my bike. Big mistake! Perhaps I should explain the road to our house was bounded on one side by an unfenced grass meadow. What upset the brute I have no idea. What is certain is that for a couple of hundred yards I just managed to keep ahead of him and then he gave up. Phew! Fear can be a mighty stimulant! But again I digress; a bad habit of mine.

In the stockmens' emporium there was a show box full of rosettes whilst certificates pasted on a feeding passage wall bore further evidence of success in the show ring. The grandfather certainly had an eye for a beast. On one occasion he spotted a young bull. At the time it was in poor condition and he gave ninety guineas for the animal.

That particular bull was named Lion and went on to win the supreme championship at the Royal. Not a bad ninety guineas worth! Never the less I was more than once admonished," Keep away from showing my lad. It's a rich man's hobby." Clearly he must have rated my chances of achieving that status as slim at best; and his judgment has proved mighty astute in that department too.

How well I recall leaning on a gate and looking across a fourteen acre field where clover had been harvested and threshed. It was just after the war and a crop of wild- white had been grown for Ridleys the local seed house. It was one of the new Aberystwyth varieties. S 100 and something—I forget which. Anyway whatever it was had realised twenty eight hundred pounds sterling. Back at the farm on another occasion about that time we looked along a range of bull pens. Hereford pedigree sales were about to recommence after the war and fourteen young bulls had been booked in. They realised an average of 110 gns. Is that all you say? Indeed it does sound a pittance until I point out a farm worker's wage at that time was £5 a week." Things are mighty rosy at the moment but no way can it last", came the voice of experience. And by no means was he alone in that conviction. Having farmed through the two depressions preceding and following the 14-'18 war few of his generation could even begin to imagine subsidies were here to stay. But then again perhaps they are not?

Next door to the blacksmith's smithy, yes there was even a smithy, there was a little slaughter house. Originally designed to supply the hall with meat it had long since fallen into disuse. After hostilities began it got a new lease of life. There were of course strict controls over the number of animals permitted for private consumption. My enquiries regarding its use drew a pointed silence from the grandfather; and judging by the somewhat brusque manner in which I was told to buzz off when it was in use I can only conclude the limit might sometimes have been stretched a mite.

Following outbreak of war food production became paramount; its days as a model farm were over. First to go was the small dairy herd and with foodstuff rationed poultry were reduced to a few turkeys, fattening cockerels and a small flock of layers. Turkey rearing was still something of an art. To try and avoid disease it was a case of installing the foster hen with her brood on an area of nice clean grass. Spring onions chopped and mixed with their food were a must to prevent disease; and young turks were super-efficient at catching disease. Did they work? Who knows? At least the turks invariably thrived. What I do know is that rather than let them interfere with the mainstream of farm work my dear old grandfather undertook many of those fringe jobs himself.

I still retain a vivid recollection of him bent over a bucket mixing a wet mash for a small batch of Light Sussex Christmas cockerels. One young rooster, a really vicious beggar with several laddered stockings to his credit, had a nasty habit of attacking from behind. Spotting his chance he launched his attack. Sadly for him our man knew of his antics and batted him neatly on the side of his napper with the mixing stick. Results were spectacular to say the very least; first a rapid retreat and then, like the wogga –wogga bird, round and round in ever decreasing circles to finally roll on his back with legs still in sprinting mode. Ah yes! Nearly forgot. For the benefit of the animal rightists among you; the bird did make a full and rapid recovery but never attempted to bite the hand which fed him again!

One final job always rounded off those Sunday morning jaunts; a visit to the veg garden no less. Vegetables in season, surely one of life's great pleasures; and one which appears nigh forgotten these days. So--- whatever happened to be in season was picked, or cut, or dug up and duly presented, with no small degree of self satisfaction it should be said, to the mistress of the house. And boy could the grandmother cook a dinner. It is always claimed Agas do something extra for cooking. There is no doubt that old coal fired range contributed a little something extra too --- even to the good lady's quite exquisite culinary skills Then again perhaps she just knew how to use it?

22. The Horse Which Climbed A Tree

Ever heard of a horse climbing a tree? No? Well not many people have, so I will tell you the story of how it happened.

On the day in question we were riding home on the school bus. As usual I was sharing a seat with my great old cronie and partner in crime. We had joined the village school together and class by class, form by form, had trodden the academic treadmill. Now here we were, aged fifteen, enjoying our ride home from the local grammar school on Mr Foxhall's luxury "Bluebird" and happily watching the world roll by.

We had just left the Ewdness stop and were passing Leavenhalls' land when suddenly, and most rudely, the peace was shattered by a great tugging of sleeves. The cause of all the commotion was a small dark-eyed boy, a mighty junior member, and he was leaping up and down with excitement. "There's a horse up a tree" he yelled at us. "Push off son before you get your ear clipped." But he persisted. "There is I tell you. There is! There is! Look! Look there across the field!"

Much against our better judgement, and no doubt working out exactly how this prankster would duly get his come-uppance, we condescended to look. "Blimey," gasped Fred "the little squirt's right!" Then at the top of his powerful lungs, "Hey Mister, Stop the bus!" But "Mister" knew us of old and he was having none of it. No Sir! Realising this I dashed to the front and, helped by the rapidly swelling clamour of excitement, persuaded "Mister" to look across the field. Bang! On went the brakes and it was fortunate there was nothing close behind or the poor old Bluebird's feathers could have been well and truly ruffled.

Out of the door, over the hedge and we were away across the field like longdogs. There were a couple of hundred yards to make and suddenly it occurred to me that friend Lane and I had got the place to ourselves. He was a good fellow that driver and true to form he had not only forbidden anyone else to follow but had stayed back himself to ensure just that. My word though it did feel lonely, and as we drew ever closer the problem loomed ever larger.

Picture a Percheron carthorse yoked to a fertiliser drill. Now picture the same horse still yoked to the drill, but dangling from his collar which, together with the shafts, was firmly lodged in the lower branches of a great spreading elm tree. There he was, he and the shafts nigh vertical, rear hooves barely touching the ground and unable to take any real weight. All very well stopping the bus and charging to the rescue but what the devil to do now we were there?

At least the waggoner who knew us both was pleased to have reinforcements. With good reason too for now the poor old horse was really struggling to breathe and clearly not going to last very long. "What the hell can we do lads?" said Bob. "Undo his belly band for starters and let his back legs come forward and take a bit of weight", said my friend without a moment's hesitation. That done he turned to me. "You climb up the shaft Ted lad, and unbuckle his bridle. And after you've done that undo his hames strap". I was beginning to catch on. "But what happens when he hits the ground? He'll go like hell!" "No he won't. I shall get hold of him and he'll never move".

Now Fred's father was waggoner on another of the local farms. "Dad" was known and much respected throughout the district and for years Fred had spent every possible moment first hindering, then helping and finally working alongside father and his beloved horses at every possible opportunity. Those horsemen all shared shared two great qualities. They were men of quiet authority and mighty self-confidence. A fair measure had already rubbed off on my friend.

"Go on", urged Fred, "He won't be any bother. You'll see". So up the shaft I clambered. The bridle was child's play; the hames strap was a different proposition. Hames, you see are the curved metal bars which hold the collar of a working horse in shape. At the top they are connected by a leather strap. Normally there is little strain on it, but with the great weight of this old boy hanging from his collar, it was a mighty different matter. That buckle, I can assure you, took some undoing. Doubtless the poor old nag's plight lent strength and eventually the strap was ready for the final pull. I glanced down. Fred was standing smack

in front of the horse. "I'm ready to pull. Stand to one side for God's sake!" No blasphemy involved I can assure you. I was scared, mighty scared, by what could happen. "Let him come. He'll be alright I tell you."

One good yank and in the blink of an eye the old boy was standing upright, back four square on terra firma. Relief, mighty relief! For he just stood there quivering, nostrils flaring and flanks heaving as he indulged the delights of breathing again. And four square in front of the great grey horse, one hand in forelock, the other rubbing his muzzle and all the time talking quietly to him stood the red-haired youth whose cool head and clear thinking had saved his bacon.

After a minute or two we quietly helped Bob to recover the drill shafts and horse's collar from amongst the branches. Then we helped to re-harness his charge and yoked him to the drill. "Thanks lads. We should've been jiggered without you" And then with a smile and a wink at Fred, "I reckon the time spent with your owld mon ain't been wasted." "What happened?" we asked him. "Damned if I know. One moment we was drilling. Next thing he was up the blasted tree. I reckon he must 'ave got whiff of a dead mole or summat."

So there you are. That is the story of the horse which climbed a tree. By the time the school bus resumed its journey life was back to normal. Bob and the Percheron were well on towards the far headland. Bob was waving and the Percheron stepping out with a renewed zest for living as the Bluebird tooted, accelerated through another gear, and tooted again.

23. Walking A Forties Winter

Why were the Forties so special? Well for one thing they were years of war followed by years of austerity. For another and, because of the war, farming which had been down and all but out during the Thirties began to boom once more. Then again the Forties were noted for winters the like of which we have seldom experienced since.

During the early Forties, the war years, horses remained the main power on the land, at least in our part of Shropshire; and throughout that decade muscle performed most of the tasks done by machinery and chemicals today. By the end of the Forties though it was clear the reign of the horse was nearly over. Farming was beginning to ride the wave of technology on which it would surge to the end of the century.

Of course changes in farming practice brought other changes in their wake. Much of that countryside now bears little resemblance to the land in which I grew up. What was then part of everyday life was in fact the end of the old way of farming. It was also the end of the old countryside and its teeming wildlife. That is what makes the Forties so special. How fortunate then to have spent countless hours walking that glorious land of copse and hedgerow, ploughland and pasture. How lucky to have had two such mentors to open my eyes to the world around me. Father did for wildlife what Grandfather did for farming. Thanks to them my recollections remain as vivid as though it were but yesterday.

Where better to begin the farming account than winter, that time when the old year winds down and the new one has yet to get going. A season when farming carries on in weather which can fluctuate between extremes undreamed of during the rest of the year. When speaking of an open spell we meant one where rain or frost or snow did not prevent land-work. Ploughing plodded quietly on. There were a few fields of autumn-sown beans and corn, but for the most part the February sun rose over a bare, brown landscape.

Whether driving horse or tractor, and of course there were no cabs on tractors in the Forties, the ploughmen never lacked company. There was always the train of crows foraging at a discreet distance in the newly turned earth. Very occasionally, quite unlike the hordes of today, a small flock of seagulls wheeled and squabbled at the very heels of the ploughman. That, my grandmothers always assured me, meant there was rough weather at sea!

Across the fields great flocks of lapwing were to be seen rising and drifting around before slowly gliding earthward again. Small flights of golden plover were to be seen taking off, knowing exactly where they were going, and taking the shortest line to get there. Pigeons, a blue-grey cloud clattered up from stubble or clover ley to circle round before alighting to rest in hedgerow trees or nearby copse. Fieldfares and redwings, usually together, circled uncertainly and with harsh, stuttering call. Flocks of tits scoured hedgerow trees and blackbird and thrush the hedgerow bottoms. Family groups of yellow-hammers and small flocks of finches feasted on lambs-tongue, dockings and thistle-heads.

Kestrels hovered and buzzards soared over the valley. Often a sparrow hawk flew straight and very high: doubtless spying his next killing run which would be at hedgerow height and executed with deadly application. Larks and meadow pipits constantly flitted from here to there as they fed on stubble or clover ley. All this to be seen by the ploughmen on a winter's day in the Forties. Now, sadly reduced in both numbers and health, the hedgerow trees are but a shadow of their former glory. And the birds? Yes, they are all still there, though not alas in such numbers. That abundance, like the trees, is but a memory!

Along a field headland a potato clamp would have been opened for the crop to be riddled, or if you prefer, graded and sorted. Pop, pop, pop of the little two-stroke as the grader rocked gently away: the clamp getting slowly, so very slowly shorter; rows of hundredweight bags steadily longer. A bitter job when an icy wind cut across the fields. Small wonder the two hardy ladies who invariably did the sorting wrapped up until they resembled Russian dolls.

Across the fields fellows were pulling and topping sugar beet, whilst others loaded it into horse drawn muck-carts. And beyond them the shepherd was driving stakes to erect rolls of netting; the prelude to folding lambs onto the wilted tops. First the leaves were eaten and then it looked for all the world as though the poor old tegs were living on bare soil. Folk riding past in cars nowadays are scandalised. Fear not! A lamb which will fatten on fresh air is still beyond genetic engineering.

Sugar-beet was the crop which saved arable farming in the thirties. It required hand labour at every single stage : sheer unadulterated hard slog! Nowadays when I watch one of the giant mechanical harvesters discharging ten, maybe twelve tons of beet into a huge metal trailer every six to eight minutes it gives pause for thought. In those few minutes it has topped and lifted as much beet as a strong man would have done in half a week's work. That machine will lift twenty acres or more in a day: five weeks work for four strong men!

It was always hoped to finish beet and tatties by the turn of the year. Seldom did that happen. A prolonged spell of rain and soon the rutted farm roads filled with water and became inches deep in liquid mud. Field gateways became seas of mud so that even with a second horse those muck-carts were just too much. Fellows pulling beet usually worked piece-rate and were loathe to pack up. With a hessian sack across their shoulders and another round their middle they used to stick at it as long as ever they could.

Sometimes Grandfather went out and called them in and found

them work in the buildings; corn sacks to repair, grain to be bagged and weighed in the granaries, floors to sweep out, fertiliser – we called it bag-muck - to sieve, last season's wool clip to bag. For waggoners there was harness to clean and brasses to shine before lending a hand elsewhere. Quite amazing how long a bit of harness could take to clean! Then of course the cowmen could always do with a hand rolling oats, or straw chopping, or slicing swedes and mangolds. Or again, there were slabs of oil cake to be broken up and fed through the crusher.

Nobody broke into a gallop; work went on quietly or occasionally a little group congregated to sort the world out and eye the rain pelting down. Invariably they were joined by one less fortunate who had been detained outside in the downpour. Most probably it would have been the shepherd and he never failed to give new impetus to the chat and banter. Water dripped from him as his collie dogs found a warm corner and set about licking themselves dry. High up beneath the eaves sparrows chirped and chirped as sparrows do on a wet day; farm pigeons preened then crooned and chortled as they sidled along a beam. All the time the rain was beating down, rushing off roofs and clattering down drainpipes. Farm cats curled tighter in their various hidey-holes around the buildings. And the old white owl? Well he had his spot high up under the roof of a Dutch barn.

All were only too happy to escape that grey soaking day, for water-proofs and wellingtons as we have them now were either unknown or unobtainable throughout the war and the austerity years which followed. Clothing was scarce and drab and invariably worn until it was both threadbare and well-patched. Almost to a man they went home with soaking wet hob-nailed boots and outer clothing and it was a real struggle to get things dried overnight.

And Grandfather? Where was he to be found? I can tell you exactly where he was. He was in the farm office tackling the mound of paper-work which arrived with the war and has continued to grow ever since. If the day was really cold he lit an old Valour Perfection paraffin stove. Whether it ever raised the temperature by one degree is debatable but at least it looked cheerful—and stank the place out! Grandfather had a good workforce and he knew it; on days like that sensible bosses kept themselves to themselves and let the world go by.

For tomorrow would be another day. After the rain it was going to take days for the land to work again but there was no shortage of jobs. Hay needed carting from outlying stacks. Take a long ladder, a great two-man job; remove thatch from part of the rick; set to with a hay knife slicing or rather chopping a face down the stack and load the loose hay onto wagons for stock in buildings and outlying yards. Loads of straw boltens required carting from the Dutch barn for bedding. There were mangolds and swedes to lead from clamps and store ready for slicing. Then there was the never ending scraping and shovelling and carting of mud from the stackyard for concrete in farmyards was still a thing of the future! Chaff and cavings from the last threshing needed shifting and burning together with fusty straw from stack bases and empty root clamps. All this was much appreciated by flocks of sparrows and finches; the cats who stalked and tried in vain to catch them; and the kestrel and sparrow hawks which most assuredly did!

After the deluge fellows needed to take spades and dig shallow trenches to drain surface water lying on winter cereals; the cereals themselves looking sad and waterlogged, complaining they would soon turn yellow with all this water at their roots. Grandfather walked the ditches to make sure land drains and culverts were working: telling me how when sugar-beet was done he would be able to start laying some of the hedges which had been allowed "to go up"; and how drains would be rodded or relaid where there were wet patches Then there was the mess the hunt had made. "There was plenty of light land they could have gone on - Blast them! I like a bit of hunting as well as the next - But why in Hell the…..?" Ah well! Perhaps better leave it at that!

Frost brought another set of problems. Threat of a hard night during beet lifting meant a rush to get every possible root off the field and into a heap where they could be protected with straw. Cover any heaps left in the field with beet tops and hope for the best. When land froze solid we could at least walk dry footed. How often the day following a hard frost dawns bright and clear. What a joy to be breathing crisp air, walking a landscape with every blade of grass and corn, every branch and twig shimmering with hoar-frost. Blackbirds, as ever, rooting in hedge bottoms; robins and tomtits with feathers puffed out to double their size. With no plough to follow, rooks and jackdaws clamoured around old nesting sites, hares went to the woods, and skylarks were loathe to fly.

A field away the shepherd was carting hay to ewes folded on kale and swedes together with their attendant starling flock. He knew the keepers were away at a shoot but there appeared to have been a miscalculation regarding Grandfather's whereabouts. His collies were fairly making the pheasants fly as they hunted the kale for a bunny. The old boy stood and stroked his moustache with one hand whilst snapping the fingers of the other one and all the time muttering "Blast him! Blast him! Blast him!" Not for nothing was he sometimes known as Blastit Davis!

When hard frost persisted it became an ongoing struggle to keep drinkers working and ice broken and cleared from pond cattle drinks. Farmers though were not the only ones who struggled. On the big pool swan, duck, coot and moorhen, even little grebe were drawn together in adversity and battled to keep a patch of open water. Invariably Jack Frost won and then they all took flight for the Severn; all that is except the poor old moorhens. Why I wonder the moorhens, for they can fly with the best? Instead they took to the land; and their chance with the foxes. Never mind, if it went on freezing the ice soon bore. Out came the old wooden skates with their steel blades and leather straps. Folk arrived from all directions to skate at weekends or at night by the light of the moon. A bonfire was always lit on the island and everyone had the whale of a time!

Few Forties winters escaped a really deep snow. In the days which followed we walked yet another world, one which was white and strangely silent. Gone were the early optimistic snatches of birdsong. Rooks and jackdaws no longer clamoured around nesting sites; partridges which had gathered in scores to chase and pair were back in coveys. For now it became a struggle for survival. When, as so often occurred, a prolonged spell of hard frost ensued that struggle became desperate.

Lapwing and golden plover rapidly migrated in search of easier pickings. For pigeons it was a case of kale and swedes or greens in vegetable gardens. Sound of shooting carried on icy clear air from all directions as farmers tried to save their crops. Rooks scoured the land with laboured flight or sat forlornly hunched in tree tops starkly outlined against a sullen grey sky.

For so many species hopes of survival rested almost entirely on the activities of man. Woodland feeding racks for pheasants, keepers carrying tail-corn to partridges, larks, pipits and linnets feeding around haystacks or hayracks and sheep cratches; clouds of other small birds, sparrows, finches, siskins, starlings, yellow-hammers, wagtails and umpteen others rose out of piggeries and cattle yards. Moorhens and partridges scuttled and took flight from stackyards. Rats, cats and foxes waxed fat on feathered misfortune! Two or three of the Forties winters exacted a terrible toll on birdlife, yet a couple of years later species which had appeared decimated were back in numbers.

On the farm, the morning which followed a heavy snow was always a bit of an event, a welcome change from routine. There was sure to be a deal of leg pulling as fellows who normally cycled or motorcycled struggled on foot. Then it was out with the shovels to clear snow where it had drifted feet deep against doorways and on pathways between buildings. Everyone awaited the arrival of the local snowplough, a great wooden "V" laid on its side and steered by a pair of handles which extended behind it. When first I recall it was pulled by two horses, then later by a tractor. In fact the horses made a better job, possibly because compressed snow from the tractor wheelings lifted the nose of the plough. After the snowplough we were part of the world again. Life on the farm settled into a new routine.

Livestock outdoors were now totally dependent on fodder and roots. As the feed wagon approached a reception committee of Hereford matrons waited eagerly at the gate. As it trundled across the meadow to the feed racks they provided an enthusiastic escort, some snatching gleeful mouthfulls of hay from the cart, others bucking and kicking up heels; then galloping ahead to be first at the trough. Dobbin just plodded steadily on, quite certain of his place in the farming hierarchy. He was the power on the land; this lot but foolish cattle! Who says class is confined to humans? Mangolds from the bottom of the load were forked out on the way back to the gate. Healthy cattle with thick winter coats, full bellies, and a good hedge to lie against at night had little to fear from the elements.

When Grandfather stood at the gate and watched this scene; or watched the in-lamb ewes contentedly pulling hay from a cratch before turning back to the roots; when he watched the last load of beet leaving the farm; or walked quietly amongst a bunch of prime bullocks running an expert hand over ribs and rumps, declaring this one a bit "tutty", his expression for over-fat, and that one needing another fortnight; at these times he radiated an air of supreme contentment. As the years passed I gradually began to appreciate these were the occasions he blessed the Almighty for having made him a farmer.

24. Walking A Forties Spring

Forties winters seldom passed without long spells of severe weather; ground frozen solid and snow which laid for weeks. Winter it seemed would last for ever. Then one day it was suddenly two coats warmer. Land was softening underfoot and the sound of dripping water could be heard. There was a touch of warmth in the sun and to celebrate the fact a hint of birdsong. Snatches of robin's spring ditty atoned for the persistent, monotonous bleat of ox-eyed tit. No songster the tit but at least he did his best. No songsters the rooks either, but this was the day when, amidst all the clamour and commotion of a great tribal gathering, they celebrated their rookery changing from winter roost to spring nesting site

Now at last we walked a land where grass and brown earth were reappearing as snow retreated to reveal clumps of that spirit of spring, the snowdrop. We knew well enough it was but a brief respite and winter would reassert itself. Cattle would remain yarded for weeks and in-lamb ewes would still require roots and hay. But we knew, and the ox-eyed tit, the rooks and the robin all knew that Spring had her toe in the door and the snowdrops were there to prove it! Slowly things began to move; frosts less severe; sun strengthening, days lengthening, soil drying out for ploughing to resume. First the horse teams, then a day or two later land could carry the tractors.

Did we realise we were watching the swan-song of the working horse? I doubt it, for in the early Forties they were still so much a part of the farming structure. Compared with the machines of today tractors were mere toys. Even so there must have been general accept-

ance that, unlike their demise following the "14-18 war, tractors were here to stay. Who though, at that time, could imagine the next ten years would witness the near total eclipse of the cart horse? There was also another factor we tend to overlook. Few, if any, of Grandfather's generation, men who had farmed through the depressions which preceded and followed the Great War, could even begin to imagine this new prosperity engendered by another war continuing.

But I digress. Soon the snowdrops were joined by aconites, hazel catkins, even the odd intrepid primrose. Leaves began to appear on honey suckle and elder; everywhere buds were swelling though it would still be many weeks before that delicate green haze tinged hedgerow and coppice. In the meantime a couple of hedge-layers and their helpers would have plenty to do.

There always came the day, usually mid to late February when we walked out across some Autumn ploughing. Wind, rain and frost had worked their magic in converting stiff clods into something which crumbled underfoot. Grandfather carefully smoothed an area, patting it flat with one foot. Then he raked his boot back and forth faster and harder until the tilth, or frost mould as we knew it, fairly flew. Whilst doing this his face took on a look of supreme satisfaction. Watching as a kid this whole performance seemed hilarious! Compare though his horse-drawn implements with their modern counterparts and you will begin to appreciate his elation.

This ritual was the signal for land work to begin in earnest. As drying winds blew and puffs of dust spurted beneath the feet of boxing March hares, rolling and harrowing carried on apace. This was followed by seed drilling. How vividly I recall looking at the number of fields, that seemingly endless acreage and wondering how on earth it would all get done. In terms of physical labour and man-hours it appeared a Herculean undertaking; but somehow it always did get done! Spring cereals, sugar beet, mangolds, swedes, kale and potatoes all got their turn.

Potatoes were quite an operation. After cultivating the field was ridged to leave it looking like a sheet of corrugated. Then pairs of planters carrying a tray of seed between them dropped the tatties a foot apart along the trenches. This done the ridges had to be split leaving the tubers beneath an apex of soil. In those days horses were unequalled for this row-crop work; I suspect it was only when tractors finally mastered it that folk really accepted where the future lay.

Whilst this great surge of activity in field work gathered momentum there was so much else going on. Down at the Sheep Cots lambing was in full swing, the shepherd and his helper keeping a round the clock vigil. Difficult lambings to help, orphan lambs to foster, mis-mothering to correct: all to be accomplished without the aid of milk substitute, tube feeders and the array of modern medication we now take so much for granted.

Back at the buildings the cowmen too had their hands full as the Herefords calved. And dodging from one scene of activity to another, the Sheep Cots, the Herefords, drilling of cereals and roots, the setting of tatties, encouraging here, urging on there, always prepared to lend a hand when the situation demanded, that was Grandfather. He had towards a thousand acres to get around, a full two miles from one end to the other, and did so on foot or cycle. There was no farm transport and during the war there would have been no petrol to run it anyway. What he did have though was quite amazing energy, a hardcore of top class workers and an uncanny knack of being in the right, or as some might have had it, the wrong place at the most inconvenient moment.

All the time the year was gathering momentum. Longer days, daffodils carrying on the good work begun by snowdrops, birdsong increasing and mercifully drowning the bleat of ox-eyed tit, King Sol gaining power by the day. Fellows could hang up their top-coats and leave home and return in daylight. More to the point they were likely to return in dry clothes and dry boots. Spring was afoot and no-one, not even the hardest of the hard bitten, was immune to her magic!

Gone now were those flocks of birds, hallmarks of the winter sky. One night in March the foreign pigeons and golden plover had flown North. Peewit and wood pigeon, yellow hammer, pipits, finches and larks had dispersed in pairs. Every acre of every field and copse, every single yard of hedgerow was disputed as they carved out their nesting territories. Pairs of partridge were everywhere. A pair to five acres was what the old partridge manors aimed for. Flocks of fieldfares and redwings still hung on; then one fine morning in early April they too were gone. Only the rooks remained a flock come nesting time.

Every Spring there comes a point when the year really does take off. A myriad green shoots appear and what was but bare earth yesterday is a living vibrant field of corn today. Wonderful! Potato ridges spring to life as tiny clusters of purple green leaves mark the site of each individual tuber. Try though I may, my pen cannot convey the sheer pleasure, the immense satisfaction of standing, as so often we did, surrounded by a newly emerged crop.

With arable crops established attention turned to grassland. Chain harrowing and rolling before the grass got growing was the order of the day. Pastures were not dressed with fertilizer, or "bag-muck" as we knew it; in fact there was precious little used at all. Only towards the end of the decade did we see basic slag applied to grassland. Invariably its use coincided with the disappearance of mushrooms.

Most farmers, urged on by the Ministry, were beginning to dress root crops with the odd hundredweight or so of "bag-muck". Unlike the easily used product of today it came in "lumpy" form: straights such as muriate of potash, sulphate of ammonia or super- phosphate. Liming did go on apace throughout the Forties, partly to compensate for the neglect of the pre-war depression, partly in response to the exhortations of a Ministry desperate for food production and victim of "lime-mania": mostly one suspects as a result of mighty generous subsidies. But I digress. Back to Spring and a highlight of that stirring season.

It was the evening the horses were turned out to grass. Mother had a great love of horses and we always went to watch. By no means were we the only ones: most of the farm fellows "would just happen to be around" as the stable door swung open. One after another eight mighty Shires appeared, ears pricked forward, a spring in their step, almost dancing on air! First a trot, then as they neared the gate to the Home Paddock they hit full gallop and sparks flew from the cobbles! Down the paddock they thundered, and round the paddock, bucking and kicking out, manes, tails and divots of turf flying: then finally onto their backs and an almighty roll, great legs flailing the air. Talk about the joys of Spring!

Nowadays when dosing of horses for worms is routine, and collection of dung from pasture is a must on the better equine establishments, I often think back to that time. How did they cope? Perhaps the secret lay in mixed stocking. Before grass even threatened to "get away' from the horses, cattle were turned on, followed usually by sheep. It was not unusual for waggoners to dose each horse with as much blue vitriol as would sit on a sixpence every Saturday morning, so perhaps that helped. Whether the Home Farm horsemen followed that practice I have no idea.

Anyway the Shires survived in tip-top condition, which is just as well because there soon followed the chain harrowing and rolling of cereals. Whilst working cereals the horsemen always kept an eye open for stones they had used to mark the nests of plover during earlier cultivations. And to ensure they did just that the owners were certain to be circling above, wheeling, diving and crying plaintively. Then there was side-hoeing of sugar beet and cultivating and re-ridging of tatties ---all to control weeds. Selective weed-killers were undreamed of at that time. Just as mixed grazing was one key factor in controlling parasites of livestock; so cultivation and rotation of crops were vital in control of weeds.

Potatoes and sugar beet in particular were the great cleaning crops. With the outbreak of war and desperate drive for food the bastard fallow, so long the ultimate weapon in weed control, had become the stuff of memory. Sugar beet was, to say the very least, labour intensive! Following horse, or side-hoeing as we knew it, a skilled operation which killed emerging weeds to within an inch or so of the plants, rows of seedlings had to be singled leaving about nine inches between each. This was done by hand hoeing, a task which invariably seemed to coincide with the first real heat of the year. It quickly re-tanned pale arms and reddened the necks of the unwary! Ideally, if weather and stage of growth permitted, there followed a second side-hoeing. After that it became a race twixt weeds and crop. Being a quick grower and excellent smothering plant the beet usually won!

Now we walked a land where Spring really was in full spate. Here was a land of infinite promise, of newly established crops; cereals which would surely grow to hide a hare in April and roots on which the hare, if allowed, would surely feast by night. Unsightly weeds like thistles, charlock and lambs-tongue had yet to reveal their presence so that pasture and arable alike looked pristine and newly minted. Fields created a multi-hued patchwork of greens bounded and framed by hedgerow and woodland creating even more shades of green : and olives and ochres which would soon turn green. England's green and pleasant land!

Some pastures were set aside for hay; others now carried the milkers or Herefords or ewes and lambs. "This", they all said " was the life"; fresh new grass at their feet and with sunshine on their backs, what matter the odd storm? There were hedgerow trees for shade and like the weeds, flies and parasites had yet to appear.

Back now to a theme I have dwelt on before and doubtless will do so again. Not only did that countryside produce a wealth of food and timber; it pulsated with a vibrant flourishing wildlife the like of which has never been seen since the end of that decade. As the winter rearguard had flown North the swallow tribe and umpteen other feathered cohorts, carried perhaps on the same southerly, began to arrive. By the 22 nd of April we reckoned to hear the cuckoo. Some heard him much earlier for the shepherd was a most amazing mimic. Our local pub could be the scene of heated debate. "You aint 'eard no cuckoo. What you 'eard was that ruddy shepherd!" "No fear it wanner. I know a bloody cuckoo when I hear one!" So the cuckoo was always early!

Now as we walked the farm cuckoos, the real thing, were everywhere. In the copses our native songsters had been reinforced by an army of chiffchafs,whitethroats, blackcaps and umpteen other warblers. Many spread out along the hedgerows to join the yellow hammers and corn buntings. So much was heard rather than seen; the tapping of ox-eyed tit, drilling of woodpecker, rasp of jay and call of yaffle (green woodpecker). From the many ponds came shrill of coot and moorhen. Birdsong was all around and above us too, for we walked beneath a ceiling of song. To really appreciate him we had to walk out across broad acres for they were his domain. The skylark!

Hail to thee blithe spirit
Bird thou never art,
That from heaven or near it
Pourest thy full heart.

On one occasion Grandfather was moved to remark "Just think of it. Not only what we can see here, but they're singing like this all over Shropshire; all over England!" Interrupting his flow with all the deflating objectivity of the young I said," I bet they're not singing over Birmingham!" The old boy stopped and looked at me. Could be trouble crossed my mind: but he began to laugh, and he laughed until tears ran down his cheeks. "No! No I bet they're not!" said he. After that whenever we walked beneath the skylarks he would stop and laugh." All over England -- except for Birmingham of course!" Mother Nature had worked her magic and man had done his part. In those days they worked pretty much in harmony. Renewal of life, both plant and animal, was again in hand. And in this kindly clime of ours we could look forward to the certainty of a harvest.

It was, or so Grandfather asserted, quite the most perfect time of year. Winter lay behind and Summer stretched ahead. To be alive and well, to be able to lean on a gate and savour the sights and sounds and scents of the Shropshire countryside on a morning in late Spring; for him life got no better than that. As a custodian of that fair land for many the long year he was no mean judge!

25. Walking A Forties Summer

Early summer found us walking another world; a world so full of warmth and daylight it was difficult to believe winter ever happened. Springtime promise of renewal was coming to fruition. Sugar beet nearly meeting in the rows, potato ridges lost beneath a sea of haulm and cereal crops already headed. Family groups and small flocks of newly fledged birds were everywhere and a walk down farm track or headland was certain to disturb a covey of partridges or brood of pheasants.

By mid June there was the chatter of cutter bars as mowers drawn by pairs of Shires laid low the grass in meadows set aside for hay. Invariably hosts of swallows and martins were to be seen hawking and feasting on the insects they disturbed. Soon these were joined by starlings bringing their flocks of young to scavenge the newly exposed sward. After the mowers there followed the tedders and swath turners to hasten drying of the crop.

Go into the field of an evening when work had finished and savour the quite indescribably beautiful smell of new mown hay. There was always the odd cock-chafer rising and bumbling around and bats hawking into the gloaming. Invariably a barn owl arrived to exploit the dire misfortune which had befallen the residents. Watch it quartering every yard, the sudden wheel, a brief hover and stoop. A few moments later it rose to carry yet another vole away to the reception party in an outlying barn.

In dodgy weather the race was on to get the crop into haycocks; miniature round haystacks some four to five feet high. Properly built and raked down they were surprisingly weatherproof. In settled weather it waited another day to be carted directly to a stack where the rick-builder plied his craft. First judge the size of the stack, or maybe stacks required to hold the crop. Next take her up level, each new course jutting a fraction proud of the one beneath. Then judge at what point to begin the easing so the final few forkfulls would complete the ridge Usually the rick -builder was a man of many skills. Invariably he could turn his hand to thatching, or hedge-laying, or draining or just about any other job on the farm. In recognition of his mastery of such a range of skills he qualified for the title of General Labourer! Talk about the ultimate in understatement.

As the crops grew so too the weeds. Imagine a world devoid of selective weedkillers. That was the Forties! If crop rotation, cultivations and subsequent hoeing or chain-harrowing failed you could say there was a problem. Another masterly understatement! Corn crops followed the cleaning crops of roots. With the national clamour for food liberties had to be taken. Rotations were extended to include more corn and fallowing was no longer an option. All this increased the workload on hard-pressed workforces. And believe me they were hard-pressed! Bear in mind too that most of the fellows added Home Guard duties to their work-load throughout the war.

In grassland thistles were the great bugbear. Ideally they had to be mown just as they formed flower heads in July. " Cut a thistle in July and it is sure to die", or so went the old saying. Like many another old saying its rhyming was the best part of it, but short of ploughing out and thorough cultivation, mowing was the only available option for containing the wretches.

With heat came flies and this caused problems for livestock. Cattle were worried by warble flies or gad flies as we knew them. When the fly was about they had but one protection and that was a hasty move. There they all were, trotting, even galloping, tails held vertically aloft; quite comical to watch but no joke for them! Gadding we called it!

Sheep fared even worse. Fly strike is a horrible thing and in warm humid weather the shepherd had to be ever vigilant. Once they were dipped the job came under control. Until then the main problem was to control scouring, diorrhea if you prefer, which creates optimum conditions for the fly. Scouring is caused by a combination of lush feeding and the build-up of gut parasites. Nowadays we have wormers to control the job. In the Forties it was a question of management. If sheep had to go onto lush pasture make sure the cattle cropped it short first.

Haytime finished and corn harvest yet to begin there was a kind of lull, a pause for breath as it were. Early summer became high summer. Waistcoated and shirtsleeved farm staff dispersed in pairs to trim hedges, or to thatch hay-ricks, or in groups to walk standing crops and hand-pull the charlock and lambs-tongue which had survived earlier attempts on their lives.

King Sol was master in his heaven and with increasing heat came risk of thunderstorms. Some said it was the underlying sandstone, others that it was the Severn: whatever the cause those storms in that part of Shropshire could be quite frightening. Of course the farmers dreaded them. If they struck when corn was at its most vulnerable, that is maximum weight of unripened grain on maximum length of unripened straw, there was only one outcome. Down she went! Lodging we called it and when that occurred the whole job became a mess. Grain ripened unevenly and, unlike the combines of today, binders did not have pickup-reels. Nowadays we have short-strawed cereal varieties and growth inhibitors to make them shorter still. If you had a particularly heavy crop in the Forties you prayed or crossed your fingers, whichever took your fancy, that straw would begin to ripen and stiffen before it caught a storm.

Of course there were beneficiaries. Crows and pigeons quickly homed in onto a newly lodged crop They arrived in their hundreds and left undisturbed played havoc. Given a choice they preferred wheat to barley with oats coming a poor third. Tom Botley was greatly in demand. Tom made his living mainly from pigeon shooting and was complete master of the art. He kept a record of his bags and many years before he retired told Father he had just notched up his century of hundreds!

Most years two or three breathless hot days in late July or early August brought another problem. They were known as " Blight Days" for the older folk swore you could see the blight. What you most certainly could see everywhere were aphids which are carriers of the fungal potato disease known as blight. I must confess to complete loss of memory regarding the measures used to control it. There were of course no insecticides as we know them now, though copper based fungicides had long been known as had the use of sulphuric acid for killing off potato haulm. What I can say with certainty is that year after year good crops were lifted and stored with relatively little loss.

As harvest, "The Harvest", drew near we walked a land where hedgerows and trees had donned the uniform rich green of high summer. As corn ripened the once green fields they bounded were becoming golden. It was a land where wood pigeon, blue-rock and turtle dove, rook and jackdaw could pass the heat of the day sunning and preening, secure in the abundance of food awaiting their pleasure.

Thick field hedges were a world of their own. Tread slowly and silently, better still tread not at all but sit wait and watch. Watch the world which unfolded before you: an insect world, butterflies, moths, caterpillars, beetles, flies, thrips, bees, wasps spiders, grass hoppers thrumming. A reptile world of grass snakes, the occasional lizard and slow-worm, and many the toad and frog. An animal world of rabbit, vole, shrew, stoat, hedgehog, weasel and rat, not to mention the fox which hunted there by night. All this without even mentioning the birdlife : all this in a thick hedge around a field of corn. That was the land we walked, fields bounded by jungles, but two species, hunter and hunted, the quick and the dead!

But back to farming where hedgerows were the last thing on Grandfather's mind. He was watching those fields of winter wheat and oats. Most likely the oats would win as they were cut when there was still a flush of green in their straw. Their grain could continue to plump and ripen in the stook from whence ancient wisdom maintained " it should thrice hear the church bells ring".

Then early one fine morning a couple of fellows, one to scythe, the other to gather and bind sheaves, arrived to open out the gateway. Breakfast finished they were joined by pairs of Shires yoked to binders. A flick of reins, a surge of muscle and away they went, rotating sails pulling corn onto chattering cutter bars, whirring of oiled cogs and chains, clicking of knotters and intermittent rattle of tines ejecting sheaves. As noise from the first team faded away down the hedge side the second started up. Harvest was under way!

Harvest always brought its own special atmosphere; urgency to be sure but something more besides. Was it perhaps a sense of achievement, successful conclusion of a year's hard work? I suspect it aroused a far deeper emotion; an ages old primeval instinct, an awareness of the difference between starvation or survival over the coming winter.

Never mind philosophy, let us recall the reality. And the reality was work: an almighty lot of work! Sheaves were the basic currency of harvest. Everything evolved around sheaves! Binders horse drawn and binders tractor drawn turning standing corn into sheaves. Sheaves being stood up together in stooks. Sheaves continuing to ripen in the stook, soaked by rain and dried again by wind and sun. Sheaves being pitched onto wagons and trundling to the stackyard behind sweating Shires; and sheaves on rubber tyred dillies pulled by a grey Fergie tractor. Evening sheaves filled every last wagon to stand overnight for unloading next morning whilst King Sol burned off the dew. Sheaves pitched onto elevators to be carried aloft into barns or onto stacks where they rested until threshing day. Then like the sheep and the goats they were separated into corn and straw!

During those early war years labour shortage must have been a nightmare for farmers. Grandfather had got double the pre-war acreage under the plough and had lost his younger men to the forces. Then again the national drive was for wheat. Minimal oats were allowed for the horses and precious little barley for malting. With few wheat varieties to choose from the bulk of harvest was bound to have ripened together. That could only have meant cutting some full early and snatching some in the nick of time. Quite a juggling act!

But back to labour. There were the older hands, laso an assortment of woodmen, gardeners and game keepers too old for military service, Land Army girls, housewives who could spare a few hours and school leavers too young for war service. Credit to the old hands for guiding, coaxing, cajoling, cursing and setting the pace! Credit to the new hands for sticking to it! Somehow, Lord only knows how, they got through those early war years. After that "P O W s" came on stream and Grandfather and his team knew they had won their bit of the war.

What about those pictures of that harvest idyll beloved of artists you may ask? Did they really happen? Did they all sit down to eat in the shade of hedgerow or stack? Did wives bring tea out to husbands and stand and chat whilst youngsters romped around getting even more sunburned? Was there the interplay of banter between the sexes? And was the world put to rights?

Did those horses hitched to a post have canvass ear caps with tassles to frustrate the flies; or maybe managed with a bunch of elder sprigs instead? And did the horses munch contentedly from a nose bag, then become restless and start to stamp and scrape the ground; then begin to twitch impatiently and finally jolt the wagon? And then did the wagonner call out "Whoa! Whoa there! Whoa you sod!"? Was it an

idyll? Of course not. It was a way of living, a way of farming which was sheer unremitting hard slog! For all that it was a scene where people still whistled and sang and had fun --------- and the Forties came close to seeing the end of it!

Watching a modern state-of-the-art combine with its eighteen foot cutter bar, massive grain tank and computerised controls: watching it mop up sixty acres or two hundred tons a day, gives great pause for thought. With modern grain dryers, short strawed cereals and growth retardants, rain, unless really heavy and prolonged, is but a passing inconvenience. In the decade I am recalling it could become a nightmare. Fields full of sodden stooks, rooks and pigeons, starlings, sparrows, mice and rats feasting on them, finally the grain itself beginning to chit and sprout. Harvest dragged and when eventually the final load was garnered it was with a feeling of anticlimax rather than elation. Everyone knew subsequent threshing would yield but clouds of fusty dust and sacks of spoiled corn.

Let me hasten to add such disasters were rare during the Forties; for if those years were notable for harsh winters they also produced some wonderful summers. That was particularly true of the war years. Truly the gods did smile on us. As Grandfather remarked on more than one occasion, "Two or three wet harvests and it could all have been a very different story my boy!"

Thankfully those harvests usually finished on a high note. Pitchers and loaders followed the last load home and cheered as the final sheaf trundled up the elevator. Next weekend the farm pigeons had buildings and stackyard to themselves as they sidled and preened or took flight to nearby stubble. Farm sparrows rifled spilled grain beneath the elevator and farm cats stalked them undisturbed.

Over the rookery its whole populace was riding a thermal; a swirling black pyramid being drawn higher, ever higher, ever slimmer, until its leaders were becoming mere specks. Then, in quite unbelievable contrast to their usual sedate flight, the specks suddenly folded back their wings to put on a display of power diving which sent them hurtling back down past those still ascending. That was the signal for the whole pyramid to collapse and reform into a great swirling, clamouring black whirlpool which finally sank and settled to chatter around their old nests. Back at the buildings the odd tortoiseshell and peacock butterfly was showing interest in the darker recesses of cart-sheds and hordes of swallows were lining the electricity wires. For them the long flight was beckoning and with them would go the summer!

26. Walking A Forties Autumn

Autumn saw us walking yet another land. Gone was the hustle and bustle, the excitement of harvest. Day length shortening, greens fading, those dry feet and shirt sleeves of summer becoming but a pleasant memory, the year was running down. If that was true of the year it was certainly not true of the work! Autumn usually developed into one long hard slog which ran well on into winter.

First those great cattle yards had to be mucked out. Lord only knows how many cart loads they held but the muck was five or six feet deep. A hay-knife was used to chop a face and the muck between it and the waiting cart was forked by hand. Then another face was chopped and so on across the yard. Depending on the distance being travelled either three or four carts were used. A chain horse was needed to get them up the sloping ramp and out of the yard. Then away to the field where the load was pulled off into heaps with a long handled muck-rake. When it came to spreading it was again a case of muck-forks and muscle.

Whilst mucking out was in full swing those two Case tractors were on with the ploughing, proudly sputtering and whining away, their two-furrow trailed ploughs turning over two to three acres a day. Before they could get cracking heaps of hedge trimmings, or brushings as we knew them would have been burned. When you smelled that smoke and heard the fluting of golden plover you knew that Autumn was well and truly under way.

Mucking out finished, the tractors were joined by horse teams with single furrowed ploughs turning over an acre a day. Ploughing was still an art form with the work set out in lands, ridged and furrowed in barrel straight lines, a joy to behold. We walked a land where ploughing carried on for weeks and months, even into February.

Compare the scene today where monster crawlers on rubber tracks pull ten-furrow reversible ploughs. Watch them turn darkness into light with their battery of headlamps and rearlamps and spotlamps as they turn over scores of acres a day. All in a few brief weeks the modern scene changes from gold, to brown and then back to green as oilseed rape and winter cereals establish.

During the Forties stubbles lay peacefully undisturbed. Those great winter flocks described in an earlier passage assembled and fed for long enough until the ploughmen finally encroached and then the clover leys became their new domain. Autumn stubbles were home to coveys of partridge which fed by day, then marshalled by the chizzucking of the old cock bird, rose and flew a few hundred yards before encircling and crouching to spend yet another watchful night. Pheasants foraged all day before strolling back to roost in hedgerow tree or nearby copse. It was a landscape where change was slow and disturbance minimal. Compared with the farming of today where fossil fuels afford hitherto undreamed of power the land we walked was one where man was still very much beholden to the vagaries of nature.

October of course was the great potato month. All the schools were given a fortnight's holiday so we kids could help with the picking. Local women added to the workforce and gangs of pickers came from the towns. Everyone had their own length to pick; we called them scoots and they were demarked by hazel pegs. Usually the pickers were divided between two rows twenty to thirty yards apart so the digger worked down one and back up the other. That way it ceased digging only to traverse the headland.

Once picked the tatties were collected and carted to a clamp which gradually extended along one side of the field. There they were tipped into a long heap, triangular in cross-section, some five or six feet across the base and about four feet high. Initially the sides were " thatched " with straw held in place by spits of soil. After a week or so the whole clamp was covered with soil to a depth of about four inches.

Every couple of yards a plug of straw was left poking through the apex to allow the crop to "breathe". Once clamped like this rain was no problem nor for that matter quite hard spells of frost; that cold snap we so often got in November." If in November the ice will bear a duck the rest of the winter will be all mud and muck". So went another old saying. Take it from me the rhyme was the best part of that one too! But I digress again. No! Only prolonged spells of hard frost could get to the tatties; and they were invariably riddled and away before that could happen.

Autumn may have brought its quota of wind and rain and work, but it brought so much more besides. By late September root fields were being walked up or driven by lines of fellows, some with sticks, others with guns. Spaniels, some liver and white, others black and white, labradors both black and golden, some hunting, others at heel, but tail-wagging to a man! Partridge shooting was in full swing again and there were plenty to shoot: for in the countryside of the Forties the grey partridge was thriving. As November arrived and leaf began to fall it was the turn of the pheasants. There they were, flying fast and high, and the sound of shooting rattled and echoed and reverberated around the woodlands..

With harvest behind him Grandfather was able to resume his market routine. It was quite a ritual. A clean striped shirt with starched white collar studded front and back, best whipcord breeches, boots and leggings highly polished—that was Grandfather. Then of course there was Bob and the trap groomed and polished to match. That old pony could really step out and they made a fine sight. For the Autumn store and sheep sales though he got out the car: south of the county really was a bit too far for the old nag!

After these jaunts he seldom arrived home before dark and was usually followed back by two or three lorry loads of store beasts. Bear in mind lorries of the Forties were miniscule compared with our modern-day monsters. On the following Sunday morning I was invariably taken to view the new arrivals. Believe me they worth looking at. Continental breeds were unheard of then and in that part of the world the Hereford still reigned supreme as a beef sire. Of course they all were horned which is difficult to envisage today.

Several trips to store sales were required to fill the yards. It was generally suspected the old boy made the job last and who could blame him. Along with market days these were the only times he ever left the farm. Prior to the war he would have enjoyed several nights away around the major shows with the Herefords. He loved showing and was remarkably successful but of course Hitler put a stopper on all that. Come to think of it I can never recall he and Grandmother taking a holiday. They could well have afforded it but I think the occasional drive over to the North Wales coast for the day during the Thirties sufficed.

Sugar beet has already featured under both Winter and Spring headings. Of course it was a major part of the Autumn scene as well. Only after tatties were finished the end of October could it really be tackled. There were no mechanical lifters in the Forties and the job was done by hand. First they were loosened by a horse pulling a beet plough between the rows. Then by gripping the stem bases two beet were heaved from the earth and the roots knocked together to remove the soil. Laid out in neat rows the next operation was to chop off the crown and leaves and throw the roots into heaps to await collection by being forked into muck carts.

An acreage of swedes and mangolds was always grown with the beet crop. Part of the swede acreage was usually left in the ground where sheep could be folded to eat them in the row. The remainder, together with the mangolds, were lifted and carted to great straw covered clamps in the stack yard. On no account must the mangold clamp be opened and its contents fed before the shortest day!

Back to sugar beet. In an open season it was not too bad. Soil knocked off easily and fellows kept dry. But few seasons remained open. Days could be wet or windy, or cold or grey; or all four together and few Novembers passed without a cold snap. When that happened the campaign was going to drag on well into winter. Always a back-breaker, beet pulling became soaking, muddy and bitterly cold as well. Hands became chapped and the beet juice prevented healing. There was a deal to be said in favour of Forties farming but I am delighted the mechanical lifters of the early Fifties consigned that portion of it to history!

By the onset of the beet campaign fox hunting was in full swing. An occasional blast of horn and the huntsman's sing-song exhortation of his pack carried across the fields as they drew roots or thicket. Pink jackets of master and huntsmen contrasted with the black or brown of the field; greys, bays and chestnuts, hunters, cobs and ponies; black and white and tan of twelve couple or so hounds; all assembled with but one thing in mind.

Fellows working the sugar beet stopped to watch and dryly remind each other that "Some buggers seemed to have got things better organised than us!". Tractor drivers stopped ploughing to run and get a better view. Waggoners had to stand and hold their teams as they all listened to the occasional yelp of hound and cry of huntsman. Then at last there was a rising crescendo, yelping and baying as the pack found and gave tongue. In a nearby meadow sheep panicked and raced to flock together in a far corner. Charlie was up and running. The hunt was on!

Threshing was a job which began soon after harvest and ran on well into winter. At that time the threshing box, or drum, or machine as it was variously known was a great feature of the rural scene. All the smaller farms employed threshing contractors and as kids at school we rushed to watch their outfits passing through the village. Usually they comprised a steam traction engine, the box itself and the driver's caravan: a timber built affair such as can still be seen at vintage steam rallies. Then though it invariably had a bicycle hung on the back ---- the driver's personal transport. The Home Farm had its own drum which was powered by one of the Cases.

Threshing boxes were amazing machines. By Forties standards they were massive. A superb creation of cast iron and quality timber they would, I estimate, have been about eight feet high and sixteen feet long Apart from the main driving wheel, which was connected to the tractor pulley by a great long belt crossed in the middle, there were umpteen lesser pullies and belts. In fact it appeared to be all pullies and belts and moving parts! After being threshed in the drum straw was conveyed to one end of the box where another machine retied it into boltens. Grain was graded through a series of riddles and screens before being bagged off from various shutes at the other end. Chaff blew out of a pipe at the side whilst a mixture of weed seed and dirt known as cavings built up beneath the box.

Before threshing could start the drum had to be levelled. That achieved the tractor pulley was engaged, the great belt began to turn and with it all the lesser pullies and belting. Gradually The revs built up, and up, and up until the machine was making a lovely rhythmic humming sound. Those boxes really bore testimony to the skill of their makers. They could thresh anything from field beans down to the finest clover or grass seed.

Once she was going everyone danced to the tune of the drum. Sheaves were pitched to the feeder and his assistant who between them cut their bands and fed the beast. That was quite a skilled task and a good feeder reckoned to keep the machine at full capacity on a uniform flow of material. If, as sometimes occurred, he overdid things, the drum gave a whoosh, the great belt leaped and clapped together, the poor old Case coughed and sputtered then gradually picked up the revs again. As for the feeder --- well he just glared around balefully from beneath the peak of his cap to take note of who was laughing!

Truth to tell a bit of diversion did not come amiss for it was a monotonous old job. Anything sufficed; the shepherd's collies hounding cats, a bag of corn falling off the sack barrow, the farmyard drake and ducks waddling homeward in line astern, the farmyard rooster hectoring his harem. It was also a filthy old job. On a still day, or with the breeze in the wrong direction the pitchers on the stack were barely discernible through a haze of dust. The unfortunate soul clearing and bagging cavings beneath the box worked in a cloud of itchy filth whatever the conditions. Dust masks were unheard of in the Forties. Like hand pulling of sugar beet threshing was best consigned to history!

When there were a lot of mice in the stack it was a racing certainty there would be precious few rats. If no mice, then excitement mounted as the stack neared the ground. At that stage rats began to appear and make a run for it. An odd terrier or two always appeared from somewhere and dealt with anything inside a ring of wire netting erected for the job. Any escaping the netting were fair game for us lads armed with sticks. What, I wonder, would our modern hygienists and animal rights activists have made of it all?

With the final sheaf and last rat accounted for the Case was shut off, the drum slowly wound down, and down, until it finally creaked and rocked to a halt as though reluctant to stop. Voices could suddenly be heard again, farm sparrows chirruping, farm pigeons chuckling and cooing under the Dutch barn, the clamour of rooks winging their way to roost. Frost was often gripping the air as the box was sheeted down in gathering gloom and robin piped a final few defiant bars of autumn song. A wash and change of clothes, a hot meal; and later a pint of beer to clear the dust. That was the best, indeed the only good part of those days!.

If Autumn brought its share of wet and grey days it more than atoned with the good ones. When those lime trees had begun to show a tinge of yellow in early August they were heralding the beginning, the prelude as it were, for Nature's grande finale to the year. One by one, almost imperceptibly at first, other species had begun to change colour. When, as so often did happen, we had a few early frosts, the whole process was hastened.

October saw the summer greens of quickthorn and bramble being replaced by a multitude of rich tints and hues. Come November wondrous shades of yellow, russet and bronze transformed mighty hedgerow elm and oak; so too their woodland brethren mingling with the gold and copper of sweet chestnut and beech, with here and there the muted crimsons and mauves of wild cherry and dogwood. For a few magical but all too fleeting windless days in November, a mellow sun rose to disperse the mists of frosty mornings and play upon the Autumn splendour of hedgerow and copse; to light up broad acres of red-brown ploughland and rekindle the gold in fading stubbles. Finally, and with evening shadows lengthening, a luminous golden light suffused the whole glorious scene; a landscape of quite stunning colour and beauty.

Then one wild night the wind raged and rain hammered down. Next day the gale continued to rage and fill the air with spiralling, tumbling, gyrating leaves. Hedgehog, grass snake and field vole felt nothing of the storm. They were long since ensconced deep inside a hedge bank. Wild duck finished stubbling and flighted to feed on frosted potatoes by night. Rats forsook the open fields and headed for the plenteous food and sanctuary afforded by outlying corn stacks and farmyards. The show was over for another year!

Before leaving that glorious countryside of the Forties, its wealth of hedgerow timber, its teeming wildlife, and by the grace of God, its abundant harvests, may I reflect once more on a few facts? No selective weed killers; no sprays for crop pests and diseases; a limited and primitive range of livestock medication; no bought-in feedingstuffs for livestock other than oilseed cake and rock salt. Fertilizer used little if at all, fertility being maintained by crop rotations involving clover leys, grazing with livestock and recycling livestock waste, or if you prefer—farmyard muck!

Now, after half a century of scientific and technical innovation, there is growing unease we may have lost rather more than we have gained. There is increasing realisation modern chemicals and their side-effects persist as part of the wider environment and as part of us long after their brief specific purpose has been fulfilled. There is a growing fear of the threat they may, or indeed may not represent. Not unnaturally there is a growing movement to revert to what was in effect Forties farming. Only it has been renamed ----- We now call it Organic Farming!!

Finally in bringing to an end this, the last of the forties seasons, may I dwell briefly on the fellow with whom I walked so many miles and who opened my eyes to the farming around me. In 1939 Grandfather was 66, an age when most men contemplate retirement; the age at which coincidentally I am writing this. Whether, with the outbreak of war, the Major asked him to carry on I have no idea. Anyway, with the younger men being called up and the country desperate for food production, he did just that. I strongly suspect he was secretly rather pleased retirement was no longer an option. Totally immersed and steeped in farming, well on top of the job, he was still a fit and vigorous man. He needed to be as well, for the next seven years, some two thousand five hundred and fifty five days would see him meet his workforce at 7.00 a.m. and do his final hurricane lanterned round of stock and buildings at 10 p.m.

Great tracts of parkland and pasture were brought under the plough to double the arable acreage. Scores of acres of bracken infested hillside too steep for arable cropping were reseeded to maintain the head of livestock. Sixty acres of tatties and thirty of sugar beet were grown for the duration. Nearly 1000 acres, two miles from end to end to be covered by Shanks pony or bicycle. That was the old boy's contribution to the war effort. Some undertaking--- some fellow! In 1946 he finally retired --- to a smallholding where for the next eleven years he milked a Guernsey twice a day and churned butter once a week. And boy was that butter! Foolish man --- well maybe? Contented man --- most assuredly!!

27. Breakfast In Paradise

Have you ever eaten breakfast in paradise? I have - many a time; and one occasion in particular springs immediately to mind. You see there was magic in the air as we sat enjoying good plain fare that morning late in April '52. Behind us a thick hedge provided shelter from the fresh breeze. Before us mile upon mile of glorious countryside called Shropshire rolled away to the distant Clee Hills. Small wonder the red grouse never bothered to go further South. And above us? Well above us was a sky full of movement and music.

And what music! Score upon score of skylarks creating their own kind of April shower, one in which notes of music fall instead of raindrops. Way above the skylarks sun and cloud and wind cavorted in the heavens to send wondrous patterns of sunlight and shadow sweeping across the scene before us. We might well have been forgiven for thinking the whole show was being staged for our own very special benefit.

One minute the Clees were bathed in sunlight standing out clear and distinct and surprisingly near. Then they faded and receded as isolated cottage and distant hamlet, church and coppice, farmstead and stately woodland each took its turn to step forward and be highlighted. Mostly it was a land of many greens but here and there reddish brown earth provided a backcloth in fields where young root crops had yet to make their mark. How many generations, I wonder, had sweated across the centuries, had hewn and ploughed, built and planted to create that fantastic landscape? One thing is quite certain: man and nature between them had crafted a view so beautiful my pen will never do it justice.

Apart from all that there was the fellow sitting beside me. Tom, you see, was my great farming mentor. He it was who introduced me to so many of the basic skills such as hedge-laying, rick-building, scything, draining, hedge-brushing, thatching, all so essential to the agriculture of the day. But there was more, so very much more to him than that. In the brief year or so we worked together he did indeed teach me a deal about farming. What is still more important, he taught me so much about a thing we call living! Take it from me, sharing a breakfast break with Tom could be an experience in itself!

For one thing he was the most cheerful of men. True he was apt to be a little hot tempered at times, usually over nothing in particular, but then so few of us ever quite attain total perfection. Between these infrequent lapses he ran a priceless running commentary on everything from farming to the general injustices of life. "Only bloody fools and 'osses sweat for a living mon". This whole performance was richly laced with humorous anecdote, rude, usually very rude jokes and all the latest local scandal - suitably embellished. Everything that lived or breathed or moved fascinated Tom, but nothing more so than skylarks.

No doubt about it; breakfast time was skylark time. The hours we spent watching, listening to and trying to count the little beggars. Tom maintained there was a pair to every acre. For me a pair to every two acres was nearer the mark, but as they were never all airborne at once it was really impossible to say. Certainly the sky seemed full of them and their music and later in the year great numbers which gathered to winter on the stubbles and clover leys would testify to their abundance.

No prima donna ever makes a more spectacular entry than a skylark taking to the air. They erupt from the growing corn as small brown bundles of musical fury. Straight up for twenty or thirty feet to pause and hover and sing their very hearts out. One little fellow staged this display but a few yards away from us. "Hi-up!" chortled Tom, "Now this young bugger really means business!" Mean business he most certainly did as he rose, hovered, then rose again. Higher, ever higher until we were lying back on the hedge bank shading our eyes against bright light. Still he soared his song gradually fading and blending into the massed chorus. Finally he hung motionless, just a speck keeping station amongst countless other specks all singing fit to burst. "By gum!" enthused Tom, "They'm fairly making the welkin ring this morning!"

But of course the larks were only the chorus, background music as

it were for the festival of life below. Wherever we looked there was life. Countless shades and tints of green together with olives and ochres testified to growing crops and leafing trees. Then there was the livestock and wildlife and people. On that one farm alone, some five hundred odd acres, fourteen of us were employed full time. Depending on the season it also carried umpteen casuals. Every other field seemed to have its team of horses, or a tractor, or just the odd soul or two with hand tools. No matter which direction you cared to look there were herds of cattle, outdoor pigs, flocks of sheep, their lambs racing and frisking at the sheer joy of being alive on that magical April morn. Then there were gamekeepers, and rabbit catchers, woodmen and estate workers. It was a vibrant, living countryside; the moment people disappeared, as we had into our hedge bank, then wildlife reappeared.

Along the hedge a wren was scolding, the activities of a stoat or weasel not entirely to its liking. Cuckoos were everywhere, their flat flight so easily mistaken for that of the sparrow hawk, which glided down the coppice side, slid over a high hedge and was gone. Further down the headland a cock pheasant was strutting and displaying in iridescent splendour. There came a sudden loss of dignity when a hare caused him to hop aside and lolloped on down the headland towards us. Closer and closer, then an abrupt halt as it sensed our presence. For a few moments it sat bolt upright, nostrils and whiskers twitching; then away across the corn, lugs laid back, going like the wind. Odd pairs of grey partridge were showing themselves in that short furtive flight so characteristic of the time of year.

There was activity along the main road too. Major road-works judging by the smoke from the old steam roller. A Midland Red bus had been held up. "He'll 'ave to toot to wake them beggars", said Tom. "They'm about got it right, them ode lads. One to work and six to watch!" Tom's admiration for anyone who appeared to avoid hard graft was always a mystery to me. His own work rate and skill were bywords in the locality. Suddenly the bus was moving again and there was a loud blast from the steamer's whistle. "Reckon that'll be tea break mon. Only bloody fools an' 'osses sweat! "

Three fields distant a horse was working in young sugar beet. In the adjacent field a grey "Fergie" tractor was ridging tatties. A nearby rookery was taking full advantage to ferry food to a host of insatiable young beaks, mighty squawking and cawing attending their efforts. Nearby a yellowhammer chanted his monotonous ditty whilst the sounds of yaffle (green woodpecker) and jay, jackdaw and magpie carried from nearby woodland and hedgerow. A wood pigeon suddenly stopped cooing and took flight from a mighty elm tree, rising steeply to clap his wings, then swoop and climb and clap again, and again, and yet again, as only wood pigeons do. Plover wheeled and called, their wing beats flashing in the sun. Tom's delight and good humour were rising with every passing moment. "The whole damn lot of 'em's got a touch o' summat this morning! Bugger me if they anner!"

By now we could see the Shorthorns heading out to pasture from the dairy. Slow progress to be sure but no doubt the grass would wait until they got there. A gypsy caravan was trundling quietly along the main road, a flotsam of ponies, traps, piebalds, lurchers and youngsters towed along in its wake. Buzzards were mewing and soaring in the distance and the beat keeper, gun under arm was walking towards us along the headland.

Tom reached for his cold tea. He carried it in a Corona bottle of pre-war vintage which occupied the small compartment of a redundant gas-mask bag of war-time vintage. Bottle and bag remained united as they were raised for one long last final swig. No parson ever lavished greater ritual on a communion chalice than did Tom on that bottle. A final decisive wipe of his luxuriant moustache and breakfast was over. We were about to rejoin the ranks of bloody fools 'an 'osses!

As we stood up Saint Chad's clock began to strike the hour. Maybe it was the sound from the church, or perhaps he too had got a touch 'o summat? For the first, and indeed the only occasion I can ever recall, Tom bared his gruff old soul a little. "Dunner think I'll bother about Paradise mon. Reckon I'll just slip down 'ere an' sit an' listen to the larks of a morning." Then, "How about you mon? You gonner join me?"

Not for a few years yet if that's all right by you old lad. But save me a seat- just save me a seat!

28. Springing The Spring Fox

Strange is it not how we vary the use of our native tongue? Take fox hunting for instance. Never did we say the hunt was meeting; it was always the hounds which were coming! And on this particular occasion it was to the Old Park farm. As always at these events tradition invariably played its part. For example, my father, the head-gamekeeper, always attended meets on the estate. Tradition of course, shaped the courtesies he exchanged with master and huntsman. Always the same old well worn dialogue --- Where to draw first? Where would they find? Which way would he run?

A more colourful scene it would be hard to imagine. It was set against the backdrop of a timbered farmhouse and a lovely range of mellow brick buildings. Snort and stamp of horse and hoof, creak of leather, hunters and cobs, ponies and hounds, far back County accents and Salopian dialect, greys, bays and chestnuts. Black and tan and white of Turk, Trueman, Badger and the other ten couple or so hounds cheerfully mingling with horses legs or exploring the farm yard. They were quite oblivious to the raving of the farm collie and terrier consigned to the woodshed for their own well being! Master and Huntsmen attired in pink. Why anything so obviously red should have to be called pink is a total mystery. Tradition again perhaps?

And whilst we are talking tradition – what about huntsmen! Over the centuries their calling has shaped them until they are almost a breed apart. This particular one was clearly shouldering the cares of the world as he sat morosely eyeing the scene in general and his pack in particular. Or was it perhaps the prospect of another happy day among the Spring Coppice briars! Never a flicker of recognition as various greetings floated his way; merely a cursory flick of whip stock to peak of riding cap.

My father meanwhile, impressively attired in plus-fours and brogues was doing the rounds. A greeting here, a few words there; then the real objective of his apparent meandering – a long crack with the terrier-men. Then, rest assured, the conversation was anything but traditional! Always great value; those lads were the very essence of rural life. Finally a chat with one or two of the beat-keepers before leaving them all to it.

Leaving them all to it was perhaps the most apt way of expressing it because for him the hunt had long since lost its magic. You see he could remember its heyday; years prior to 1914 and again in the Twenties when the estate was laid out for hunting. Hedges were maintained to perfection, field gates and hunting wickets all in perfect working order and come October every last strand of barbed wire was taken down! After darkness fell on the night before a hunt every fox earth, badger sett, drain culvert, indeed any hole large enough to allow Charlie to get to ground would have been stopped by the beat keepers using brushwood faggots!

Hunts were not just about killing foxes. They were great social occasions and the whole countryside joined in with a will. Anyone who could muster a nag and ride to the Meet did just that. Fields were huge and there was a host of followers: lads playing truant from school, folk from all walks of life, some on bicycles, others on foot, many from the local towns. For those unable to attend the Meet it was a case of keeping eyes and ears cocked for sight or sounds of hound and horn; then one mad dash to try and get a view of Charlie! Come opening time it was certain to be the talk in all the local pubs; where they found, where they lost him, why they lost him, where they found again, where they killed, who came a cropper here poor chap and who went arse o'er tit there serve the bugger right!

In those days hounds could run for miles without being whipped off at every bit of bye-road for fear of motor traffic. Huntsmen and field could ride hell for leather across country, taking hedges as they came to them. "Don't over ride the hounds gentlemen": was a saying which held real meaning. It was exhilarating stuff and Father had loved it. "Nowadays", he was apt to remark sadly, "It's nothing more than a day's hacking. Good luck to them for trying; but none of these people have ever seen a real hunt. Nor are they likely to again --- more's the pity!"

After leaving the Meet we walked homewards along the Eastern rim of the Severn valley. For the most part its steep slopes were heavily timbered, mainly oak. Alongside us though a great swathe had been felled during the war. Way down below us in the bottom ran the river and its attendant railway. Where the floor of the valley widened sufficiently there were strips of farmland. There the railway stole a short cut leaving the poor old river to go the long way round!

By now we were approaching a small outcrop of rock which jutted out, and with the standing timber gone, provided a most wonderful viewing point. To my great surprise – and not inconsiderable pleasure, Father suggested we should wait here and watch them draw the bottom. It meant waiting some time of course but that was no hardship for the beauty and tranquillity of the scene stretching out beneath us afforded ample compensation. Hard to imagine this was the valley which cradled the Industrial Revolution though less than a mile upriver the famous Iron Bridge bore graceful testimony to the fact. A strip of rough grazing below us was still known as The Foundry Field.

Odd dwellings were scattered along the river banks. By the standards of today they were quite unbelievably isolated; their only access a footpath or rutted and muddy cart-track. According to local lore they had been built to service the barge traffic which once plied the river.

After the initial tree felling rabbits had been cleared to allow regrowth of saplings. Their absence was much appreciated by the resident briars which registered vigorous approval by climbing up through the brash left from tree felling. Soon the whole steep bank was clothed in great breaks of them, some higher than a man's head.

Small wonder the poor old huntsman had looked less than happy. In actual fact he was a cracking good fellow and his pack too was a real working outfit. To tackle that lot it needed to be! He had dismounted and was going to take them through on foot. Of one thing you may be quite certain --- both he and his white breeches were in for a tough old time!

What immense fascination there is in watching a pack of hounds at work. Always a hard-core of honest grafters who will tackle the toughest going and always a fringe of slackers quite happy to let them! Much like humans really! Splashes of black, tan and white appear, muzzles raised, sterns wagging, then back into the undergrowth again. Odd whimpers and an occasional yap as rabbits or hares are started.

Their whole progress can appear sporadic and almost aimless as they cast around for a scent. Overseeing it all though is that fellow in pink with the voice and the horn, a combination of sound only the truly initiated and his pack can ever hope to understand.

Years following hunts and controlling the fox population on the estate had left Father with an uncanny insight into the ways of the animal. Having watched for twenty minutes or so he quietly remarked "If they don't find very soon --- then Charlie's not at home". Hardly were the words uttered when there was a rusty-brown flicker some fifty yards ahead of the pack; then a brief glimpse of the fox as it crossed a few yards of open ground.

"Just keep still" said father "She'll come this way." That initial brief sighting, even at distance was enough to convince him it was a vixen. We had a marvellous view as she came uphill towards us. No panic. No rush. Just a steady lope threading her way between breaks of briars. Now lost to view in dead ground created by the rough terrain, now visible again, a marvellous sight, every detail of her black-rimmed ears, white tip of brush, becoming clearer by the moment. Once more she disappeared into dead ground some forty yards below us. "Don't move a muscle", whispered Father who was standing less than a yard away from me. I stress the distance because she suddenly breasted the bank at our very feet almost brushing our legs as she passed between us.

A tall quickthorn hedge bounded the woodland some thirty yards or so away. Having reached it she stopped, turned around and, would you believe it – Sat down! She appeared completely unaware of our presence, or the little groups of foot followers straggling along the path. Her whole attention and her every nerve was riveted on the pack which had sprung her and they had yet to utter so much as a whimper. Apparently satisfied she roused herself to make off across the Long Pool meadow with that lovely deceptive gait which covers ground so effortlessly. Father later told me it was by no means unusual behaviour by a hunted fox. Over the years he had witnessed or been told of many similar incidents.

Now though, it was a case of bringing on the pack which was still some distance from where the fox had lain. Normally quietly spoken he never-the-less possessed an extremely powerful voice: and this he employed to some tune! View Hoying. Loo-Loo-Loo-Oning. The odd melodious whoop ---- and all this directed at a pack crashing round in thick undergrowth at least two hundred and fifty yards distant! It

seemed impossible it could work. It certainly took time, maybe a quarter, perhaps even half a minutes, but first one, then another hound lifted a head. Suddenly they were heading uphill towards us. Then the leaders hit the scent and began to give tongue. A fantastic melody of yelps and bays grew louder by the moment and became almost deafening as they surged past us, then checked and cast around at the hedge before hitting the line again and streaming away across the turf.

Little groups of foot followers had hurried along the path to get a better view of proceedings. They had been well and truly rewarded with a most amazing exhibition of yelling-on. You could tell by their faces that few, if any of them had ever seen or heard anything like it before.

Glancing at Father it dawned on me that not only had he lifted the pack, but in doing so had worked himself up into a fair old state! Red in the face and fairly bristling he had well and truly got the bit between his teeth. Now having lifted the pack he began to enquire the whereabouts of the whipper in. And take it from me he was not whispering! "Where the Hell's that whipper in?" he was bellowing and by this time thoroughly enraged. Followers who had been so keen to get nearer the action were now equally intent on putting some distance between themselves and this tyrant in plus-fours who by now was striding back along the path in search of his quarry. Distant groups could be seen shouting and waving to someone as yet out of view. Impossible to hear what they were actually saying but their body language afforded eloquent translation. "For God's sake and your own lad – Get a move on" Sure enough the whipper-in appeared, still on the Coppice side of the hedge, pelting along beside his mount, red in the face and blowing hard. Very hard!

He was clearly intent on reaching the gate into the meadow before Father got there and just made it by a short head! "And where the devil do you think you've been?" roared Father. "And why in Hell aren't you mounted? You should have been up here to collect them! Whipper-in! Whipper-In" he roared --- "why you couldn't whip a bloody cat in!" All the time the poor lad was trying to get his foot into a stirrup. After several botched attempts he finally succeeded, swinging into the saddle and making good his escape in pursuit of the distant pack and even more distant fox.

Suddenly we had got the place to ourselves. Foot followers were legging it back to vehicles parked at the Old Park, the pack was far away across the Big Turf and heading for Stockton End, the Field straggling in their wake, and far behind the Field the Whipper-in. Now there was silence! A silence broken only by the crackling of dead branches as way below us the poor old huntsman struggled back through the briars to recover his mount.

Father took a final look around and then headed for home. There was a swagger in his step and he was, without any shadow of doubt, mighty pleased with himself. "Doesn't do any harm to let them know where they stand occasionally" was all he would say. I knew exactly what he meant and he had certainly done that to some tune. Where on earth had he learned to lift hounds like that? "Practice. Practice. And more practice! You see when I was first involved in it hunting was a big thing on the estate. So was shooting, --- And the two didn't mix. Though I say it myself two or three of us became mighty expert at lifting hounds off a beat where there were no foxes to somewhere they would find. You know we could take them for far enough!" "But didn't the Huntsman know?" I asked "Oh he knew all right! But I'll guarantee he was the only one who did. And he wasn't going to say anything because he knew damn well we seldom failed to put him onto Charlie. Oh no!" He knew the score alright!"

29. Blue - Grey Cloud

"Come on! Hop in the car. There's something I want you to see."

If memory serves correctly that would have been 1945 or thereabouts. Pointless enquiring what we were going to see: so try the next best ploy. "Where are we going then?" "Over to the Crowgreaves".

Reaching the farm of that name we turned off the tarmac and down a farm lane. Nearing the end of it we drove very, very slowly up to a field gateway. Looking through the bars of the gate we had an excellent view across a large field. My father was a great believer in surprises and this time he really had excelled himself.

What should have been a large green expanse of clover ley now looked blue, or perhaps to be strictly accurate blue-grey. There appeared scarcely a square yard without a hungry wood pigeon feasting on it. Indeed they were feeding greedily right up to the gateway itself, but a few yards away from us. It seemed every pigeon in Shropshire must have congregated there.

We sat and marvelled at this nigh unbelievable sight for long enough. Finally Father said "Now just watch this!" With that he quietly opened the car door and got out. Immediately the woodies nearest the gate clattered into the air. It was as though he had lifted the corner of a blue-grey carpet, a carpet which continued to lift and rise as the alarm wave surged away from us. Half way across the field it began to falter, only to accelerate again as he once more clapped his hands to lift the remainder into the air.

This was no flock of pigeons; it was a cloud of pigeons; a twenty acre cloud which took long enough to stream out high over the Worfe valley before circling and settling in the Badger woodland on the far side. What a spectacle; a once in a lifetime, never to be forgotten spectacle, the like of which few are privileged to watch

Now came the inevitable question. " How many were there Dad?" "Goodness only knows! Tom Botley reckons at least fifty thousand!" Now Tom was no amateur. Pigeon shooting provided a goodly part of his living and he ranged far and wide over Shropshire. He explained to Father he had based his estimate on the acreage of the field and density of birds on the ground. Rest assured he was not exaggerating!

Tom had made several attempts to shoot them without any real success. That hardly seemed possible for where pigeon shooting was concerned he was the ultimate professional. In the early fifties, some years before retirement, he once told my father he had just notched up his century of one hundred bags, his best day being just over 250 on a field near the Wrekin where he had run out of cartridges!.

30. Ratty

Few, if any, animal revolts us humans more than the rat. Perhaps this revulsion reached its peak during the days of the '14-'18 trenches. How well I recall my father describing how cold their feet felt on his face whilst trying to snatch the odd hour's sleep. He also recalled an attempt to save a loaf of bread from them. It was hung by string from a beam in their billet. That would fix them it was agreed but come morning there was only the string! Perhaps it is their ability to get so close to us, to transmit disease, to invade our dwellings, our very privacy, to say nothing of our food which so revolts us.

And what so-and-so use are they is the question so frequently asked. Surely the same could be said about other pests, the fox and indeed the grey squirrel? Perhaps if Ratty sported a nice bushy tail instead of that sinister scaly looking appendage we would think more kindly of him? But then Foxy provides a deal of sport. What better sight or sound than a hunt in full cry? Though it is true there was at least one stately home where the male guests of house parties could gamble of an evening on the rat killing abilities of terriers, poor old Ratty generally has less to offer and is usually restricted to providing a bit of fun for lads with sticks and assorted dogs.

On the other hand he can provide quite a spectacle when making the occasional mass migration: one great mystery by any standards. It is certainly not for want of food and the numbers involved can only mean them gathering from over a big, big area. What triggers it? How is it communicated? A milk tanker driver told a farming friend of mine how, on one very dark morning, his headlamps lit up an even darker patch on the road ahead. Driving closer he realised it was rats, not scores, but hundreds upon hundreds of rats crossing before him. Later that evening my friend, who farmed but a quarter mile away, went into a big building. Realising at once he was not alone he shone his torch around. Where ever the beam landed it was reflected by eyes; eyes on ledges, eyes on beams, eyes on machinery, eyes everywhere. He quietly came out and shut the door and, sturdy fellow though he was, confessed to being frightened. Next morning they were gone.

Only once have I personally seen rats migrating. They were in a corn stubble moving parallel with the foot path; clearly excited they were constantly hopping above the stubble and apparently oblivious of my presence. How many? Certainly scores, possibly hundreds but for the most part hidden by long stubble. Another massive migration was witnessed in the Via Gellia by an uncle. Looking across the valley, he said the whole floor of the wooded hillside appeared alive and moving. As in my case they were clearly excited and ignored a human presence.

Going back to my youth—and that was a few years ago—the countryside was a paradise for rats. Thick hedges and hedge banks, harvest which lasted weeks with fields full of stooked corn; the harvest stored in stacks or Dutch barns; field ponds, feed racks for game, granaries and hessian sacks, livestock on every farm, a pigsty and poultry run at nearly every cottage---- the list could go on, but Oh Boy, what a bonanza! And did Ratty make the most of it.

Perhaps this little story told by a retired farm worker best illustrates the point. Fred worked on a farm which boiled potatoes for pigs. A boiler house lay some distance from the main buildings and between them ran, not a rat run, but a veritable track. A local estate was offering a bounty of one half-penny per rat so Fred and a workmate decided to cash in. Armed with sticks and a hurricane lantern they returned after dark. Having got inside the boiler house Fred's accomplice took one look around and stated that no way was he staying in there; so he was told to get outside, hold the door and stick a boot in the bolt hole. Fred then laid about him with his stick and the result of his efforts was duly presented to the gamekeeper. That gentleman was busy making snare pegs beside a blazing fire. One by one he cut off the tails, threw them on the fire and counted one hundred and thirty seven rats! Then he gave them back the bodies and counted out five shillings eight and one half pence (27p) which was the equivalent of a day's wages at that time.

Of course Ratty has not been without his problems. Apart from natural enemies like foxes, and stoats, many districts had a professional rat catcher. Most households and every farm kept a cat and a stroll round the buildings at dusk was certain to disturb the owl. Outlying corn stacks were trapped and how well I remember carrying the hurricane lantern on those forays. Threshing days provided a great opportunity for levelling the score with Ratty: wire netting around the stack, terriers and pitchforks within, lads with sticks and the shepherd's collies without. A great time had by all apart from Ratty.

Then of course there was poison and indeed gassing. Arsenic was an early standby and strychnine would have been widely used. Rodene, a poison based on white phosphorus, or so I was told, was the first brand I can recall. Then at last came warfarin and everyone thought Ratty was a gonner. Throw in combine harvesting and grain storage in vermin proof buildings and silos; also removal of hedges; absence of potato, swede and mangold clamps; disappearance of livestock from so many farms and cottages and it is easy to see why his numbers are down, at least in the countryside.

But a resilient soul is Ratty. Concern that he is coming to terms with modern poisons has led to talk of Super Rats. Certainly he is very much alive and flourishing. It is even possible that at some time in the future Ratty himself may yet look back with nostalgia to a golden era when there were humans on the planet, and the comfortable living they afforded. Surely no animal, not even the cat or dog, has ever forged such an advantageous relationship with humans? Loathe or love him— and few do—you can but admire him!

31. Whoa Fergie Whoa

Before beginning the real story I had better describe what a harvest field was like in the days before combines and pick-up balers, or indeed straw-burning. You see we used to have a machine called a binder, a wonderful invention which not only cut the corn, but tied it with twine into bundles known as sheaves.

It was pulled by a pair of great cart horses, those of the arching necks, glistening muscle and switching tails. There it used to be, chattering and whirring and clicking away, sails sweeping endlessly round - tumbling the standing corn across the blade and onto the canvas belting to be carried up and into the binder only to reappear a few moments later neatly tied into sheaves ready to be flung out by the tines and left in rows marking the binder's progress.

There was a beautiful and ever changing pattern in a harvest field. It began to emerge the moment the first cut was taken round the outside of the crop. Then round again, and again, each time the area of standing corn that little bit less, but always retaining its original shape. So too the rows of sheaves faithfully following the line of the hedge. Not for long though, for very soon a gang of workers appeared. They set the sheaves up on end, six or eight together, depending on the type of crop, to form rows of stooks in which the corn continued to ripen and dry.

Rabbits were another feature of harvest. We always hoped the binder would start and finish a field the same day because when that happened, and the standing corn was reduced to the last few rounds, the conies began to bolt. Once committed to the long dash for safety across new stubble they could be chased and run down by the fleet of foot. Rabbits hotly pursued by young or sometimes not so young fellows, were to be seen flying in all directions. You can imagine the cheering and hollering and general excitement. Dear old Connie never failed to berate us for being "a cruel pack of young sods". Nor did she ever fail to overcome her moral qualms in time to cycle home with a rabbit hanging from her handlebars.

By the time the binder finished the last round and left the scene it was usually well into the evening and we were left to stook the remaining sheaves in a stillness which is nigh unknown today. It was a stillness "so quiet you could almost hear it" and voices carried clearly across the fading scene. A field of ripening corn would have been transformed to create the subject so beloved of artists. Given the inter-play of sunlight and shadow, the challenge of perspective and contoured symmetry presented by rows of stooks who could possibly blame them? But I am getting carried away! Now you have some idea of what a harvest field was like we can get on with the real story!

You see it was the time when muscle was giving way to metal on the land. A team of mighty Clydesdales were still the main power in the harvest field but there was a usurper in the offing. He was a sleek little fellow, grey in colour. By comparison with its large and lumbering predecessors Harry Ferguson's new tractor was unbelievably small and compact. Needless to say the waggoner eyed this newcomer with an ill-concealed air of condescension. Seldom did he miss an opportunity for extolling the virtue of four legs at the expense of four wheels. By no means though did he have things all his own way for the Fergie's handler was equally devoted, indeed one might almost say besotted by his charge.

A great flow of banter developed and everyone joined in with a will. Eventually this culminated with the waggoner declaring in no uncertain terms "Any damned fool could drive a tractor". "Show us 'ow then", we yelled. Poor old Harold! Too late he realised the trap had been artfully laid and baited and he had walked clean into it. "Go on", we urged, "you reckon any damn fool can drive a tractor. Get your arse on that seat an' show us 'ow!"

Harold was nothing if not game and he climbed aboard the Fergie. To his eternal credit he did so in a way which had us wondering whether he might yet have an ace up his sleeve. Had he got behind a wheel during those years in the army? But no! Once installed the chickens strolled home to roost. Apart from placing two hands on the steering wheel and a boot on each of the rest bars he had not the faintest idea of what to do. "Go on then! What yer waitin' for?" "Well show me 'ow to start the ruddy thing then or I canner show yer."

To call it an evil leer would be unkind for he was anything but an evil fellow. Shall we just say the Fergie's handler radiated an air of supreme smug satisfaction as he leant over and prepared the waggoner for take-off- or should I say blast off? "Right now! Get your left boot on that pedal. That's it. That's the way. Now keep it pressed down 'till I tell yer. Now that's 'ow we start 'er up, 'an that's 'ow we slip 'er into gear," said he carefully selecting top. "Right now keep yer foot on that pedal 'an then lift it nice an slow like." With that he pulled the throttle wide open and bawled "Right lift yer foot," simultaneously taking evasive action reminiscent of a Spanish bullfighter. Results were immediate and spectacular as the grey Fergie came out of the blocks like an Olympic sprinter.

I dwelt earlier on the great beauty of the harvest scene. It's doubtful whether this aspect crossed Harold's mind as the little tractor took charge of proceedings. That Fergie had a mind of its own! Away it roared, demolishing a whole row of stooks, bucking and rearing as first front, then rear wheels bounded and leapt over heaps of sheaves. Other sheaves caught in the tread of the tyres and flew past his ears. And what of Harold? I'll tell you. He had got his feet braced on the foot bars and was half standing from the effort of pulling back on the steering wheel with all his might. And all the time he was roaring, "Whoa Whoa! Whoa then you bugger!"

At first it looked as though Harold and his mount would go the length of the field and take the far hedge. Then, whether by the waggoner's efforts, or its own evil instincts, the grey Fergie began to carve great circular swathes of devastation through the stooks. "Whoa!" yelled Harold "Whoa you bugger!" By this time rabbit chasers had become Fergie chasers and there was more than a hint of alarm. Panic would be a more appropriate word, for it was not so long since the Fergie's handler had impressed everybody by cornering at speed and turning the little beggar clean over. On that occasion, thanks to timely intervention on the part of the Almighty, he and his passenger had both been thrown clear.

Eventually, and to much acclaim, someone finally managed to leap aboard behind the waggoner and lean over to switch off the ignition.

Mighty relief all round! As for Harold, he just sat there, a little ashen faced perhaps, but still managing a grin. All the rabbit chasers turned Fergie chasers stood or staggered around gasping for breath. As for the older hands, they were far too relieved to say much, but rightly berated us all for "A pack of bloody lunatics! 'An who the 'ell did we reckon was going to restook all the corn?"

"Not me at any rate!" Harold, God bless him, had had the last word. "I've got me 'osses to see to! They canner be switched off 'an left like ruddy tractors!"

32. Go Fetch The Cockerel

Harvest was in full swing on the Bank Field with sheaves being pitched from stooks onto a wagon drawn by a Clydesdale. Our steady progress downhill between two rows of stooks was taking us close to a complex of red brick buildings, known as The Dairy, which housed a herd of pedigree Shorthorns.

Only mention the word pedigree in farming circles and a form of elitism immediately begins to taint proceedings. We may all have worked on the same farm but those chaps at The Dairy certainly regarded themselves as at least one cut above us lesser mortals. Never was this more apparent than at harvest or hay-time when, admittedly with a fair modicum of diplomacy on the part of management, it was suggested they might care to put their shoulders to the common wheel; and this despite the fact we were getting hay or straw for their blasted pampered cows. They duly appeared, all in their own good time of course, with the air of fellows who knew only too well they could not be managed without. We for our part, at least in our more charitable moments, regarded them, to put it politely, as somewhat over-indulged.

Given this background you can imagine the reaction when the head cowman, appeared round the corner of The Dairy, not with a pitchfork, but leading the bull. Not any old bull you must appreciate, but The Bull, the pride and joy, the very flagship of the Shorthorn fleet. In all fairness he was a big fine burly fellow and had dressed to match the occasion. With natty straw hat and a smart smock he could have been parading his charge in a show-ring! Between them he and the bull were cutting a fine dash. Worse still they were both mighty well aware of the fact and swaggered away down the field knowing they had scored heavily. Even Tom, seldom known to be lost for a word, could only mutter sourly, "Big 'eavy bloke with 'is big 'eavy bull!"

Beyond the hedge at the bottom end of the Bank Field lay a lovely grass meadow surrounded by majestic hedgerow elms. That was where the cows were and that was where the mighty duo were headed. From our vantage point on the bank we were, like it or not, going to have a grandstand view of proceedings. Of this our man was only too well aware. Talk about stage management!

To say the cow was co-operative would be the understatement of the year. She fairly pranced across to the gate to greet her intended. "Ah well. That's it 'int it?" said the wagoner. "He'll be ruddy insufferable time he comes back". But that was not it! Quite unbelievably, to our utter amazement ---and supreme delight I might add, William was displaying a complete lack of interest. " Too good to last " we told each other "The sod 'll get his act together in a minute!" There was in fact one heart-stopping moment when the blighter did actually attempt to honour his side of the contract.

But attempt is all it was, and a pretty pitiful one at that! Feigned indifference on our part was rapidly giving way to intense and highly vocal participation in proceedings. It would be quite impossible to say which looked the more forlorn and dejected, the bull or his handler. By now it was abundantly clear we were to be spared those withering looks as the triumphant pair swaggered their way home. Our man was clearly waiting, no doubt praying, for some form of minor miracle........ Divine intervention as it were. He waited just too long though for the cow, clearly an animal who knew her own mind, mounted the bull!

Disaster! The ultimate humiliation! Resounding cheers from the boys on The Bank and it was clear our deadly duo were going to have to make a run for home. Now leading out a ton of Shorthorn virility which would grace any show-ring was one thing. Running thegauntlet leading a great hunk of overweight and dejected impotence was an entirely different matter.

Nor was there any shortage of excellent, albeit ill-intentioned advice." Try exercising the sod. Wouldner do either on yer any harm come to that!" " A pint of linseed tea twice a day..... That's what 'e needs!" " Get shot on the useless bugger and get yourself a Friesian!" This last from Tom, back to his old self, and quite the cruellest of thrusts. Just as well our friend had the bull in tow or there could well have been bother! Finally they both made good their escape round the corner of The Dairy. Could he possibly have conceived at that moment that even greater humiliation awaited?

Pitchforks it seemed had barely to tickle sheaves to send them leaping and flying to the very top of the load. Even the shepherd who had somehow slipped up badly enough to find himself pitching was in high good humour. Mick the Irishman alternated between his rendering of The Woodpecker's Hole and how he used to milk more cows by hand, 'Tan tose lazy beggars do with all tat fancy machinery!" Meanwhile Tom crooned monotonously on about the nigh unbelievable virility of Friesian bulls.

But suddenly there was silence! No! Surely it couldn't be! It damned well was though!

After all that and the cheeky blighter still had the brass-neck, the sheer gall to show his face again.

There, before our very eyes, as large as life, and with an assumed air of supreme nonchalance was our friend heading off down his garden path; it was the ultimate, the supreme show of defiance. It was also a mistake of monumental proportions on his part for at the end of the garden was the chicken run.

"Haw! Haw! Haw!" bawled the wagoner in a voice which would have been heard in the next parish," He's going to fetch the bloody cockerel!"

33. Two Tun The Aacre

It happened in the days of yore when the Minister's men organised events for dissemination of farming skills. And jolly good a lot of them were too; a fact borne out by their general popularity. This particular get-together was held on a large and well run Lincolnshire farm; and the subject of the day was winter wheat.

Following the customary introduction of farm and host, hardly necessary for the latter was a mighty well known local character, business of the hour began and time honoured procedure came into force. All troop behind Ministry and our Ted: out of farm yard, along rutted track, through gateway to assemble in corner of a newly harvested stubble. Why the devil, I can imagine you thinking, was this event being staged after combining rather than seeing the standing crop? The straight answer is - I have not the slightest idea but can only imagine they would all have been too busy harvesting their own to attend here. Anyway proceedings now followed the standard Q and A format twixt Ministry and host.

Q. "So what did this one follow Mr. S?"

A. "This'un came aafter sugar beet."

Q. "And what was the variety Mr. S?"

A. "We put this'un in with Capelle"

And so it went on- Seed rate, fertiliser rates, type and timing, spraying for weeds, and anything else besides. Finally the all important

Q. " And how did it come off Mr. S?"

A. "This,un did two tun the aacre!"

Now back in the time of which I write that was some going. Scarce

an eyebrow raised though for our Ted was a highly esteemed character of known integrity. General acclaim all round. He could farm a bit could our Ted! So all move on in straggle formation at plod pace to next stubble. And the next. Invariably the same answer to the final question, the punch line as it were, Two tun the aacre!

Niggling doubts had by this time been kindled. All a bit too good to be true and there was much muttered conferral in the ranks en route to the final field. Came the punch line once again, but before Ted could reply came a loud and sarcastic interruption.

"Two tun the aacre then Ted?"

The trap had been artfully laid and the bait taken. Now it was sprung.

"Noo, noo, Oh noo!----Noo not this one. Noo this,un went to make them others do two tun the aacre!"

I did mention earlier that he was a character.

34. Knowsley Interlude

In 1911 my uncle left home and went to Knowsley. Just how that came about is perhaps worth recording. It appears, or so the story has it, that the Lord Derby of the day had a bee in his bonnet about an impending shortage of young head gamekeepers capable of carrying on the traditions of the great shoots.

At that time, and indeed right up until, and in a few cases several years after the second world war, many of the larger estates ran what was called a bothy in their kitchen gardens. This was home to varying numbers of young fellows ambitious to become head gardeners. It was a form of tutelage or apprenticeship and it produced some remarkably able men. His Lordship's idea was to extend the system to game keeping. In Alex McLauchlan, his head keeper, he had the ideal tutor.

Just how that worthy had come to be at Knowsley is a story in itself. Lord Derby, who happened to be looking for a new head keeper, was shooting with the Duke of Devonshire at Chatsworth. So impressed was he by the Duke's man, one John McLauchlan, that he asked him whether by any chance he had a brother who might be interested in the post. That was in the morning. At lunchtime John had himself driven to the local Post Office and sent a telegram to his brother who at that time was station master on one of the Liverpool sub-stations.

On receiving same brother Alex scribbled a reply for the messenger boy, removed his station master's head gear, sent it skimming across the lines and headed for Knowsley. Early in the afternoon Lord Derby received confirmation he had got himself a new head gamekeeper.

But back to the bothy. To qualify for acceptance to that establishment applicants had to be six feet tall and the son of a successful head gamekeeper. Perhaps there were other conditions but since Grandfather and his brother Isaac, a leading figure in the gundog world, had been meeting and socialising with the McLauchlan brothers at Crufts for some years Ted's acceptance was probably something of a formality.

In those days everything at Knowsley was done on a vast and lavish scale. House parties, shooting, breeding and racing of bloodstock, the whole place throbbed with activity and interest. Poaching of his Lordship's game was also on the grand scale for there were numerous coal mines in the area. Usually they poached in gangs of six or eight, but occasionally came out mob-handed and looking for trouble. Ted once told me how he and five others sat still and mighty, mighty quiet in the shadow of a hedge one night as twenty four walked past them.

On another occasion creaking of the top strand of a barbed wire fence told them that a party of six had climbed over it and were heading their way. One of the older keepers leaned across and whispered in his ear. "Just thi' get one down Ted lad an' I'll 'it t' bugger!" He nearly choked trying not to laugh out loud and give the game away.

With his extremely powerful physique my dear old uncle had quickly established himself in this department. Those set-tos were pretty rough and in that area the first thing to look out for were clogs flying. With their pointed metal toe caps and horse shoe style iron shodding they were a nasty weapon. Because of the numbers involved a chain gang was kept by the keepering staff for conveying their captures to the local police.

Ted's ability with both rifle and gun quickly revealed itself and he and another keeper called Nat Barnes shot on all the bye-days. At that time the bye-days accounted for some four thousand head of game! When duck, snipe or woodcock were needed for the Hall, and that was often, he was invariably given the job of getting them. Snipe, by the way, were usually shot on a local sewage farm!

Every autumn there was a roundup of swans on Knowsley lake. Exactly what the purpose of this was I cannot say. Perhaps it was the kind of swan upping which takes place on the Thames. Whatever it was Ted always maintained that if you really wanted to end up black and blue from ankle to thigh, then separating fully grown cygnets from their angry parents was a sure fire way of doing it! Whilst on the subject of Knowsley lake it is worth mentioning the method they used for controlling pike numbers. It was both novel and highly effective. Live-bait were attached to the necks of empty bottles (cider bottles were ideal) using a wire trace and short length of line. A boat was quietly rowed the length of the lake and baited bottles were popped over the side. Just how long the bottles were left I have no idea, but by all accounts it was a simple matter to retrieve them on the return journey as even a large pike was unable to keep one submerged for very long. As a means of controlling the pike population it was apparently very effective.

As on so many estates cricket was taken extremely seriously and Ted excelled in the bowling department. One day Lord Derby sent for him and said that Lancashire would be prepared to take him onto their ground staff to train as a fast bowler. Was he interested? Uncle declined the offer but continued to play good cricket and when working in Norfolk some years later toured with the Nomads of that county.

During the shooting season Lord Derby's itinerary took in the very cream of the great sporting estates across the length and breadth of the land. On these trips Nat Barnes invariably acted as his loader. One year Nat had a broken arm and Uncle took his place. It was a unique opportunity, not only to see the great shoots, but also to watch the best shots of the day. He watched De Grey, said by many to be the leading shot in the land, on numerous occasions. It was reported in the press that he frequently had five or six dead birds in the air at one time. The most Ted ever saw him with was three, just possibly four, and believe me that was shooting of some order!

So much more could be related but these few anecdotes give some idea of the full and varied life enjoyed by so many estate employees of that era. The path for advancement did exist for those with the determination and ability to follow it and the majority of estate owners adopted a liberal attitude and actively encouraged them to do just that.

Finally a couple of short stories just to round this account off.

Derby Day

During his days at Knowsley my uncle courted and eventually married a vivacious young lady, a descendant of the great John Peel no less, whose father managed Lord Derby's bloodstock stud. John Griffith's position afforded a unique and intimate insight into the racing world. So when Grandfather Sharpe received the letter from a dutiful son advising him that a certain horse was going to win the Derby and to be sure and get some money on before the odds shortened--- he did just that.

Perhaps I should digress a moment to explain why the Knowsley people were so certain their horse would win. After weaning the colts were grown on in long paddocks. Frequently, and entirely of their own volition, a bunch of them lined themselves up at one end and then raced like the wind to the other. Future winners quickly revealed themselves and this boy was a dead cert.

Back to the betting. Every thursday afternoon heads of departments on the Apley estate gathered in a room at the Hundred House for a meeting with the agent. Perhaps coincidence but an itinerant bookmaker always visited the village at the same time. My grandfather was never a betting man. On the other hand he was never a one to do things by half. That bookie must have thought it was his birthday when this inexperienced punter laid a "pony" at odds of 8 to 1.

Perhaps I should explain what was meant by a "pony". Just as we talk of a "grand" these days, meaning a thousand pounds, so at that time a "pony" denoted the quite hefty sum of twenty five pounds. It got its name from the fact that it was the cost of a good sound horse at that time. Put another way it was several weeks wages and you may rest assured my grandmother, a somewhat formidable lady, would have been anything but happy about the arrangement.

So what you are asking was the final outcome? Well the horse duly ran, and won, with consummate ease. Grandfather, doubtless with a spring in his step, and not least for having proved a point on the domestic front, set off to meet the bookie and collect his winnings.

But alas! No bookie! That fellow was never seen in the district again.

Oh! I nearly forgot. You still want to know the name of this wonder horse. It was none other of course than the great Hyperion himself.

Horses for Courses.

Given a fair wind and a fine evening the head coachman, a mighty well known character around Knowsley, collected his roach pole and a bucket and walked the short distance to his favourite swim on the lake. Having got himself comfortably settled he set about reducing the population of small roach. A bob of the float, a lift of the rod and another silvery wriggler came flying to hand to be deftly unhooked, tapped on the head and popped in the bucket. In due course the evening's catch was carried home to be boiled up for his flock of laying hens.

One evening he was unfortunate enough to be spotted at this harmless occupation by a couple of well dressed dames who happened to be strolling that way. As senior members of the female staff at the Hall they were by no means unaware of their own importance in the general scheme of things;

"Oh I say", exclaimed one to the other in a voice calculated to carry, "Just look at that beastly man killing that poor little fish"

"Madam", boomed the beastly man in a voice guaranteed to carry,
"   If only he had kept his bloody silly little mouth shut!"

35. Problem Boy

Picture the scene. A Suffolk smithy steeped in local lore, its owner one great local character. Enter one lady driving a decidedly top of the range 4x4 towing horse- box to match. Clearly this was a lady used, shall we say, to exercising a degree of authority. So when the blacksmith announced his intention of turning the mighty well-bred passenger into the paddock until he was ready to shoe him --she was horrified.

"Oh my Gawd! Do'nt even think of turning him out. You will never,simply never ever manage to catch him."

"Well ma'am tis only marnin' and you aint a'goin' to collect un till arter four. No ma'am he'll 'ave to go out. Now do'nt you worry ma'am he wo'nt be no problem!"

"Well", said she," One only hopes you know what you are doing."

Totally unimpressed the smith extracted a little bottle from a waist-coat pocket, dabbed a drop of liquid onto the palm of a horny hand, rubbed the droplet between thumb and forefinger, gave problem boy a sniff up each nostril, opened the door and out he went.

"Well," said she "I shall be here to collect him at four thirty and I only hope he will be ready." Clearly she did not expect him to be ready and doubtless would have a few well chosen words to say on the matter.

So shall we move on to the appointed hour? Re-enter one immac-ulate conveyance; re-enter one overbearing lady fully expecting to find the smith and apprentice making forlorn and futile attempts to collar the problem boy. Rest assured she was well and truly rehearsed on the lines of told you so and had you only taken the trouble to listen to me!

But wait. What had we here? One newly shod nag clearly happy with life. And one blacksmith, back pointedly turned in her direction whilst he put the finishing touches to a set of harrow points. Job done and his own point made he turned to madam.

"Well shall we drop the back an' 'ave him in ma'am?"

" Oh yes! But I simply ca'nt imagine how you managed to catch him."

"Oh twarnt no problem ma'am", said he taking Neddy's bridle to lead him aboard.

"Well you certainly will not get him in like that". Authority was being restored! " There's only one way and that is to blindfold him". And with that she produced the necessary article.

"No call for that ma'am. No call for that" once again fishing in the old waistcoat for the magic bottle. Repeat performance. Ritual rubbing of thumb and forefinger, a whiff up each nostril, then up and into the trailer toddled Neddy quiet as a lamb.

Flabbergastered – completely, utterly flabbergastered!

"Well that is unbelievable. Quite, quite unbelievable": and she was still marvelling when a sudden thought struck her.

"I say, you could'nt possibly, possibly let me have the formula for that potion could you"?

"Well why not ma'am. Whynot? Tis nutt'n more'n a mix o' tom cat piss an' pepper!"

36. A Day For Rejoicing

There was always a healthy rivalry between neighbouring farms. And what better focus for this than the laying of a boundary hedge between Astoll and the Crowgreaves? Apart from dividing two of the best farms in the district it also ran to meet a busy little road which was known locally as the Rabbit Run. In those days workers from local farms pedalled the Run in numbers. Clearly the laying of such a hedge was destined to be the subject of great interest. Mighty great!

Now Mick the Irishman had laid hedges at Astoll many a long day and despite advancing years, not to mention some pretty fierce competition, he was the man chosen to fly the flag. Yours truly was the man assigned to help him and with the crass naivety of callow youth deemed this something of an honour.

One fine crisp winter's morning the job got off to a highly impressive start. There was Mick stomping and strutting around in shirtsleeves and waistcoat overseeing everybody and everything. First there was the tractor driver to instruct as to exactly how and how many and where he wanted the heaps of stakes laid out. Then he had to show me exactly how he wanted them pointed and topped, and just how he wanted the hedge brushed out and sided up and how the brushings and trimmings would have to be heaped and burned. Altogether he was a busy fellow and chose to ignore the various waves and greetings coming from the Rabbit Run. After all Mick had his reputation to consider. Local comment regarding his age had clearly not passed unnoticed!

Preliminaries completed to his satisfaction, Mick set about the business of plashing and laying and driving of stakes like a man possessed. Keeping up with the old rascal was a real struggle and after three or four days the Rabbit Run was retreating nicely into the middle distance. The Gaffer paid frequent visits and was clearly delighted by developments. He and Mick engaged in serious debate which always gave way to prolonged head scratching, rearranging of caps and much nodding and smirking in the Crowgreaves direction.

After the initial burst it dawned on me the pace was slackening; and so too did the reason. As the Rabbit Run receded it became increasingly difficult for its more critical users to assess our daily progress. Then the weather turned cold. Day after day a bitter north-easter blasted scuds of snow out of a leaden sky. It was the kind of weather hares take to the woods and small birds are loathe to fly. With any other fellow this would have induced greater activity if only in the interest of generating heat. But Mick was not any other fellow. No Sir! Mick's reaction was to pull his cap further down and tug the collar of his long black jacket ever higher. Eventually the sole remaining signs of life were a pair of pink ears, twinkling blue eyes and a battered pipe. Only when its owner stopped smoking twist and chewed it by way of a change was the poor old pipe allowed a rest.

I mentioned this odd behaviour to Tom. "Oh arr", replied that worthy, "the old devil goes torpid in cold weather. Sort a' like a fish in a frozen pond. 'Cept when he's on piece work o' course; then the ruddy artic wouldner stop 'im"If nothing else we had plenty of time to look around and observe the toings and froings of the world. Bob Fields for example. Bob was one of two waggoners at the Crowgreaves and he was taking his week's holiday. Sugar beet finished and spring work yet to begin it was safe for Robert to take a week off. Most of the farm fellows "took it when they could be spared" And usually just pottered around home or made the odd trip to pub or town.

At nine o'clock each morning Bob was to be seen cycling along to the Crowgreaves. He would have claimed he went for a bit of a chin-wag with the stockman or whoever happened to be around the buildings. We all knew he really went to see his horses. Than he cycled home and disappeared indoors for an hour or so. When he reappeared it was to cycle in the opposite direction. Mick ran a running commentary on all this.

"Look ye now at owd Bob. Look now he canna leave them damned horses to inyone else. 'An what if he dropped down dead tomorrow? Thwat difference would it all make?"

"Hello! Hello now! Our Robert's away to the Hundred House. No! No be gad he's turned for Bickbury. It's the Seven Stars for him today then."

"Now thin! Now thin! It's Bridgnorth for Bob today. Look how he's all dressed up. He'll be havin' a pint and a haircut in the town. That's for sure."

Then one morning Bob reappeared immediately after returning from the horses. "Be Gad" said Mick, "but Robert's soon out again. An' all dressed up too! Must be Wellington for him today. But no! Hang on boi God! He's headed this way. Now get stuck in Idward, get stuck in lad. Pritend we haven't seen him!"

So get stuck in we did. Mick was plashing and stake-driving for all he was worth. "That's it Idward, that's it lad. Get stuck in. Pritend we haven't seen him!" We surely did more in the few minutes it took Bob to walk down the headland than the rest of the morning put together. All the time Mick was peeping from beneath the peak of his cap and I knew he was timing the moment he would suddenly spot the waggoner and hail him like a long lost friend, at the same time pushing back the old cap and mopping sweat from brow.

It didn't quite work out. Our visitor had stopped about thirty yards short of us. As Mick had said he was all dressed up, in brown as it happened, from stylish trilby right down to polished leather leggings and boots. He was a splendid looking fellow too and had a great bass voice which could be heard from far enough across the fields.

"Bad news gentlemen!" He boomed. With that he paused long enough to have us hanging on his next utterance. What new misfortune had stricken this long suffering world! Had those Russian tanks finally begun to roll?

"HIS MAJESTY KING GEORGE THE SIXTH IS DEAD"

There was no doubting the solemnity of the occasion, or indeed the sense of loss, so far as Bob was concerned. Doubtless he was expecting these sentiments to be wholeheartedly endorsed and returned by this section of the Astoll workforce. So it must have come as an almighty shock when Mick flung back his head and gave vent to a sort of strangled yell, most difficult to describe, but possible to interpret as either a laugh or a wail.

It was the last reaction anyone might have expected and from the look of Mr Fields was not being received any too kindly in that particular quarter. Nor was the sequel going to be! For I knew the signs only

too well. Hedging axe would be waved aloft in one hand, then he would smack his thigh mightily with the other before giving way to peals of uncontrollable laughter. Fortunately he had turned toward me whilst giving vent to his initial bray.

"Shut up you damned old fool!" Such rudeness was normally undreamt of but something drastic was called for. It did the trick. "Thwoy? What's the matter? "You look round and you'll see what's the matter" Mick sneaked a long peek back from beneath the brim of his cap. Then turning to face the waggoner he flung his arms wide. Consternation and concern were etched in to every wrinkle and line of his weather-beaten face. "Be Gad! But that's tirrible news Bob! Tirrible news indeed. A fine owd king to be sure. The Lord only knows how the Divil we'll mange without him".

Our visitor bestowed the cold eye on this performance for a long and ominous few moments: then, turning on his heel, stalked away up the headland. "Thank ye Bob! Thank ye for letting us know," yelled Mick after the broad and very expressive back. Then turning to me, "An thank ye lad, thank ye very much. He's a big powerful feller is that, 'an it doesn't do to be the wrong side of the like of him. I reckon oi owe ye one!"

Owe me one? Owe me one? Was I hearing things? Presumably not, because whenever I saw him in the pub after that Mick was either heading for home in the deuce of a hurry, or so totally engrossed in the nearest game of darts or dominoes as to be oblivious of everything else around him. Anyway if the poor old King's passing served no other purpose it certainly did make Mick's day. He forgot the cold and beavered away in great good humour. There were frequent pauses to refill the old pipe with wafers of John Peel dextrously sliced from a stick of twist.

These pauses were real social occasions. Mick was in expansive mood, and in expansive mood he was the greatest of company. With renewed activity the old fire was blazing merrily again. Mick beamed and puffed on his pipe whilst pulling forward the tails of his long black jacket the better to warm his backside. Then a few sprightly steps from a jig and he cackled and chortled away. "Who'd iver a thought o' that owd bugger dyin'! Fancy havin' to go and leave all thim jewels and robes an' palaces an' what have ye behind. Come the end o' the day lad, oi reckon he's no different from the rest on us after all!"

37. That Little Man In A Mac

He was often to be seen as we walked down the High Street on our way from school. Sometimes he rode a bike; occasionally, very occasionally, he drove a little Austin Seven; one of the real old "sit up and beg" variety. Usually though he was on foot and for some strange reason was often to be seen taking stock of the world from a vantage point right smack in the middle of High Street itself! You must appreciate that in the 1940's the word volume had yet to come into use as a description of traffic.

It made no difference if he was walking, riding or driving, nor for that matter whether it was raining, hailing or shining. Of one thing you could be quite certain ---- he would have been wearing a flat cap and a riding mac! Clearly he was a fellow of some standing. Like the good shepherd he knew his flock and was known of them. Always a nod and a smile, not only for the adults, but for any of us youngsters brave enough to say Hello.

Friday afternoons my father usually came into town. Officially he came to visit the Estate Office, but of course there were other small matters to attend to. High on his list of priorities would have been a lengthy chat with an old friend of his. Invariably Father ran Percy to ground on the steps beneath one of the Town Hall arches and that is where I often used to join them.

Looking back what an oddly assorted pair they were. In tweed plus-fours father stood large and powerful, proof apparently against anything the elements might send. Percy by contrast was lean, so often appeared pinched from cold, and spoke with a strained voice.

Both had served in the trenches and both had, as the saying of the day expressed it, caught a packet. Father was the lucky one; he sustained shrapnel wounds but by 1921 was able to throw away his second stick and start work once more.Percy alas had been badly gassed and would never work again. When health did permit he fished and was an absolute ace in that department. For a youngster those Friday afternoon sessions on pike and perch, chub, trout, eels and otters were something to savour.

One of those occasions I recall quite vividly; for after we had taken leave of Percy and were walking on down the High Street I took the opportunity to ask Father about that little man in the cap and riding mac. "Good Lord", said he, "Don't you know who that is? Why that's the Town Clerk".

What, I asked, was a Town Clerk? More shocked disbelief, and then because we had arrived where his car was parked, we stood on the pavement whilst he patiently explained the many duties and responsibilities of a town clerk. Father often revealed quite amazing insight into matters one might easily assume held little, if indeed any, interest for him. And did he do all that himself I enquired? Of course he didn't. Oh no! He had a small staff and some rooms in the Town Hall were set aside as offices.

Now for the rest of this story we need to skip a few years --- a little over thirty to be exact! Father had a few matters to attend to in town and we had spent the morning there. Business completed we disentangled ourselves from the car park on the old Fair Ground and then queued in a stream of traffic to negotiate the narrows of the North Gate. Whilst we were waiting there he said, as though on impulse, "Turn down Whitburn Street. There's a sight you ought to see".

So down Whitburn Street it was. Years since I had been down there and doubtless the old sub-conscious was projecting an image of the green hillside which would soon appear beyond the houses. "Good God! What the devil is all that?" Modern municipal architecture seldom aspires to beauty and the unsightly creation imposing itself on my mellow pastoral image came as something of a shock. Sunlight flickered and shimmered on glass and harsh red brick and reflected from roofs and windscreens of the attendant sea of cars lapping around its walls. We managed to pull over to take a longer look.

"Thought that little lot might cheer you" said Father. Then, "do you by any chance recall that nice little fellow in the cap and riding mac we

used to call the Town Clerk?" I remembered him very well indeed. "I don't for one moment suppose you can remember me once telling you what his job was? About how he had a small staff and offices in the Town Hall?" On the contrary I could remember only too well.

"Well that little lot is what he has grown into!"

So what had altered?

"Nothing really" said he. I knew the tone only too well ... a subtle blend of sarcasm and banter. "No that's the clever thing about it all. Roads still get maintained. Property gets repaired. Rates and rents still get collected and so do dustbins. Of course the railway's gone, buses are few and far between and the hospital looks like closing." Sarcasm was by now beginning to get the upper hand of banter! "But of course we do have a chief executive. None of that old town clerk nonsense. And the chief executive has a host of minions!" Then after a long pause --- "Take a good look son --- Because those are your new masters!"

Why mine and not his crossed my mind? Presumably age was finally on his side! Anyway as we drove on down the Squirrel bank I was beginning to come to terms with what the intervening years had achieved in transforming the little man in a mac. Recollecting him brought back memories of another fellow---that lonely guy who used to stand on the steps of the old Town Hall.

I was older now, thirty years older, and with increasing age had come ever growing appreciation of the quite staggering sacrifice people like Percy had made. I reflected on the shattered health, the abrupt agonising end to a promising career in the Post Office. I thought of the fiancée who had so badly wanted to stand beside him: and how, quite wrongly perhaps, he had refused to marry for fear of leaving a young widow, or worse still a young family unsupported. And then, reflecting on the pittance a grateful nation lavished on its one time wounded heroes. I could not help but compare it with what we had just sat and looked at.

As we crossed the bridge over Sabrina's mighty river, turned left at The Falcon and headed out of town it dawned on me, that whether by accident or design, dear old Father had contrived to bring home to me the enormity of what was, and for that matter still is happening in this country. Those words came back then and have continued to do so ever since. "Take a good look son ---- Because those are your new masters!"

By now we were approaching the Town's Mills, driving alongside that lovely stretch of river flowing so tightly beneath the towering ramparts of High Rock. It was some time since either of us had spoken. Really there was little need, for I was close to my father, and had a pretty shrewd idea the lines his mind was running on. Perhaps more to confirm my intuition than anything else I put the question to him.

"What do you think your old pal Percy would have made of it all?"

"Funny you should ask that. This was one of his favourite stretches of river you know". Then almost fiercely "I'll tell you what he would have made of it all". Gone now both banter and sarcasm. Age had done much to mellow Father but I had touched a raw nerve. Usually so kindly and genial his face was suddenly suffused with anger.

"Percy would have been feeling very, very sick!"

38. Severn Stream

The Severn by which I grew up in the Forties was a river of infinite variety. Quiet reaches of deeper water flowing placidly seawards, flats we used to call them, gave way at intervals to shallow fords or runs where it cascaded over gravel or coursed through rocky channels. Those were the places where the power of a big river could really be felt.

It was my father who opened my eyes to the teeming world of tiny creatures for which the river was home: he did it by gently pulling a clump of ranunculus weed from its gravel bed and laying it in the shallow water's edge. Watch the scores of shrimp, larvae and nymph for which it was both sanctuary and larder making good their escape. Then think of the myriads of silt and stone dwellers also browsing on algae, diatoms and a host of other minute life forms. Another world of which so much remains unknown. A watery jungle. But two species------ the quick and the dead!

He explained how this host of tiny wriggling creatures was the mainstay, the bedrock as it were, of the whole huge diversity of life supported by that great river. So many of them were destined to eventually emerge from their watery home to hatch into an infinite variety of fly life. Mayfly, dragon and damsel fly, umpteen species of duns, caddis and stonefly; not forgetting of course the myriads of midge which made their presence well and truly known of a summer's evening. Creatures of ethereal beauty, all in their season destined to share our world for but a few brief hours during which they would mate then form clouds of spinners drifting slowly down to lay their eggs in the river from whence they came. A perpetual renewal of life.

A summer's evening saw fish rising everywhere; great shoals of bleak and dace dimpling the tail end of fords and score upon score of chub creating rings on the flats as far as the eye could see. Here and there a trout and many a samlet feasting on both hatching and spent flylife. Samlets, or parr as they are often known, are the young of the salmon and work gradually downstream, feeding and growing until finally they don their silver mantle and enter the mighty ocean. Meandering seaward they would have encountered great bars of silver, their very own kind, forging upstream to the spawning grounds which gave life to them all. Beneath the surface pike and perch stalked their lesser brethren whilst yet more species foraged and harvested the river bed; loach, gudgeon, bullhead, ruffe and minnow; flexing roach, sinuous eel and lamprey.

Then there were the water fowl. Duc k, swan, dabchick and dipper all feasting on underwater vegetation and animal life; kingfisher and heron plying their fishy trade; broods of newly hatched ducklings, the young of coot and moorhen all feeding on insect life. And along the bankside there was an endless rollcall of what we normally regard as land birds; wagtails and chaffinches, dunnock and wren, flycatcher, warblers and so many more, all hunting that wealth of insect life along the river's edge.

So far no mention of the furry fellows. The river was home to water rat—for indeed they were water rats in the Forties---- and haunt of otter. What I wonder has become of Ratty of Wind in The Willows fame? Perhaps he is now Water Voley? How ironic the generation which watched over his demise should have changed his name.

Finally the airborne brigade. Those scores of bats which emerged of an evening to join forces with hordes of swifts, swallows and their martin cousins all gorging themselves on the winged banquet rising from the river below. What a wonderfully vibrant festival of life that old river supported

At one time the river had carried barge traffic. Finally the iron horse forged its way via tunnel and deep cutting to service the trade and industry of its glorious valley--- and replace the barge. A number of isolated houses scattered along the banks could only have been built to service the barge traffic. One in particular I recall built against and indeed into a sandstone rock face. No water, no electricity, its sole access a footpath through a wood, it was known not surprisingly as Rock Cottage and housed a family with several growing youngsters.

Doubtless those old walls could have told a story or two!

Coracles of course were before my time though my father told of many an hour spent watching their owners, the Ironbridge coracle men, absolute masters of that watery domain as they netted for coarse fish or night-lined for eels. It is difficult to understand why the word coarse ever came to be used to describe fish of such diversity and beauty. Perhaps it had something to do with their culinary qualities. With the notable exception of eels, and just conceivably the firm white flesh of a perch well fortified and disguised with herbs, they leave a deal to be desired. During the war my mother occasionally stuffed a pike with sage and onions and then baked it to grace the family table. Invariably pronounced delicious it none the less fell rapidly from grace once rationing ended!

Speaking of the coarse fish takes me back to a favourite swim beneath the branches of a great spreading oak. It was home to an ever willing shoal of ruffes, Jackie-ruffes we called them. The old float used to bob and jig away for long enough until one of the little spiny fellows finally managed to pull it down. On one never to be forgotten occasion though it did slide strongly down and away and I tightened into solid resistance. After a good old struggle it was landed, a glorious vibrant creation of bronze, green, orange fins, bright red gills and flaring spines. A mighty perch of one and three quarter pounds, which, it being wartime duly landed in the frying pan. A couple of even larger ones were caught and returned in quick succession. Then no more. That shoal of big perch left the swim just as suddenly as they had arrived and the Jackie-ruffes were free once more to bob and jig to their hearts' content. Goodness only knows just how many times I fished the swim but that was the only occasion I ever caught a perch there. Such is fishing!

There were plenty of good roach but I never caught one more than ¾ pounds. Being of tender years and with the Severn a deep and powerful river flowing between steep banks my fishing was restricted to safe areas such as sandy bays and shelving shingle and probably for that reason I never got amongst them. Anyway whilst I watched a float of an evening Father was trying for a salmon. On this particular occasion I noticed he had stopped fishing and then quite unexpectedly he appeared on the path behind me. Not only was it far too early for him to have packed up but he had changed out of his waders. Very strange. He was also unusually quiet. None of the usual fishy chatter.

After hovering around for another half minute or so he confessed to having a little problem. Must have broken his rod crossed my mind. But no. Somewhat sheepishly he showed me his hand.

One of the three hooks of a large salmon treble was deeply embedded up to and even beyond its bend smack in the ball of his thumb. Any sane man would have been making tracks for A&E. in a hurry. Not Father. Oh no! That was to be the last resort.

"Have you got your knife?" I fished in a pocket and produced same.

"It's not very sharp" I ventured.

"Never mind. Just keep it tight against the hook"

So I had a go. Have you ever tried cutting live flesh with a blunt instrument? It was hopeless and if truth be told my heart was not in the job.

"Damned if I'm taking this to the doctor. Trouble is getting a grip on the other two?"

Bear in mind hooks have barbed points and he would be pushing against them. Just how the devil he managed it I shall never know but there was a mighty grunt, an even mightier roar and fifteen stone plus of head-keeper was bouncing up and down, leaping feet into the air whilst waving the treble in triumph. And never a swear word throughout!

Coming back to the roach, how well I recall standing with Father on a high bank and looking out over a fast run. Clean shingle was fairly sparkling beneath the rippling surface of shallow rushing water, but there was more besides. Flashes, scores of flashes as though silver plates were being turned to reflect the bright sunlight. For a few moments we were completely baffled--- and then it suddenly dawned. We were watching a huge shoal of big roach flexing and twisting as they stripped algae from the river bed.

Kingfishers were a constant source of fascination. Apart from their amazing plumage, surely unique, almost out of place in fact in this temperate land of ours, the distances they flew was always a bit of a mystery. Whilst feeding young they must cover countless miles. And come to that how rare an event it was to see them actually fishing. Surely with all the fish in that old river there must have been a few good fishing spots within a couple of hundred yards of their nest. Ah well, it all remains a mystery yet I can still see the iridescent jewel which alighted on my rod and began preening itself whilst I was fishing for the spiny fellows beneath the great spreading oak.

As I grew older trips to the muck heap in search of brandling worms became a thing of yesteryear. The worm had given way to the fly. Shallow runs provided great sport with chub, dace, the odd bleak or samlet and very occasionally a trout. Percy Price had given me a little split cane brook rod which together with a length of un-tapered silk line and an ancient brass reel found in the attics comprised my kit. Later I was given a venerable Greenheart fly rod by a maker named Ramsbottom. Never heard of him? Nor had anyone else but despite its years that was by far the most perfect casting tool I ever fished with. Seldom did I fish alone for we had a Black Lab name of Sweep who, completely of his own volition, decided I needed company. Wading at my heels he took a mighty interest in proceedings and in no time was retrieving played out fish which he held until they were unhooked. With his soft gundog mouth he damaged them less than a human hand might have done and they were returned in perfect going order. When activity was slow he amused himself by sticking his head underwater to collect stones which he carried and dropped on the bank. Something of a strong hint you could say!

It soon became clear the head of trout was much reduced by comparison with my father's young day. As a youth he could fish a dry fly and regularly take two to four brace of an evening. Those days had gone but never the less my over-riding ambition was to land a big Severn trout. Chance came one evening when there was a nice hatch of mayfly. A really good fish was rising at the head of a run, steadily mopping up everything that came his way. Of course we had no dry flies, let alone a mayfly, but with that genius for improvisation with which some folk are blessed Father took a large teal winged wet fly and roughed its feathers backwards and outwards until it resembled a hackled dry. He tied it on and said "Try that!" A decent cast, a strong swirling rise, a shower of golden spray and two pounds of brownie headed off at speed. Disaster! He was gone and with no real strain applied. Examination of the cast revealed the awful truth. The knot had pulled. Poor old Father. A look at his face and I felt for him. Alas it must be confessed I felt even more sorry for my self. In a lifetime of fishing I doubt he had ever done that before or since. I never did catch my big Severn trout but it was a lesson which I bet has saved me many a fish since!

Most seasons a really whacking specimen appeared on at least one of the fords. But those trout were not interested in flies. They were usually there for one and occasionally a second season and were all too easy to spot. Their presence was signalled by a small fish scudding across the surface in a series of desperate leaps, the final one disappearing in a fierce swirl. When they were on the feed that could happen several times in an evening Guessing weights can be a dodgy game, especially for fishermen, but on one occasion one of those big fellows chased a small fish straight between my feet as I was wading water too shallow even to cover his back. He made good his savage capture before flapping and wriggling his way back to safety despite, it has to be confessed, my best efforts to prevent him. That fish would certainly have tipped the scales at 5or 6 pounds. Unlike their lesser brethren those big cannibals never fell for a salmon fly or small devon minnow. Clearly their years had not been wasted!

No matter how slow the fishing there was always so much to watch and listen to. Swans nested on several of the fords, always a respectable distance of say half a mile apart. Invariably there was a constant probing and assertion of territorial rights. How often the cob from the upstream pair was to be seen drifting down with the current until a great white feathered galleon launched itself from the downstream territory. Then suddenly there was a huge explosion of activity, whistle of mighty wing beats, paddling feet beating the water, as the two great birds became airborne. Both flew swiftly up river until the pursuer reached the top of his territory and landed in a flurry of spray thrown up by outstretched feet and wings. Settling back in the water there always followed a great display of headshaking and nonchalant preening: in fact every sign of satisfaction at another job well done! Meanwhile the transgressor flew on upstream to land near his own nesting site.

Our friend Ratty, or should I say Voley, enlivened many an evening. If things were quiet on the fishing front then he was much in evidence. Sometimes they carried a piece of vegetation in their mouths but, apart from the odd scratch or sprucing of whiskers, life appeared completely and utterly devoted to swimming from somewhere to nowhere in particular. Then of course that other animal of mystery and enchantment. There was always evidence of otters, occasionally their spraint, frequently the large scales of a chub amongst the empty mussel shells on a shingle beach providing evidence of a recent feast, but seldom were they seen. It was always a thrill, almost a privilege in fact to catch sight of one fishing; a head suddenly there then gone again without so much as a ripple, only to reappear once more twenty or thirty yards downstream.

On one mighty fortuitous and never to be forgotten occasion I was able to watch one actually fishing. Standing on a high bank I was gazing down to the rocky riverbed visible through the clear grey-green water of early Spring. Something scarcely more than a shadow was moving down below there, surely a salmon or a big pike? It moved swiftly upstream into shallower water and the shadow suddenly had legs Now it was darting rapidly from one rock to the next, for all the world like a terrier dog pointing then hounding a rat from one sanctuary to another. Then a head broke the surface and it was holding another head in its mouth. Swimming briskly ashore our friend disappeared to feast on the eel in solitude.

That day was memorable for another rare sighting. Whilst fishing further upstream I spotted one solitary small bird flying steadily up river towards me. There was something about its flight. On it came following the line of the bank and no more than twelve feet above the water. Surely it could not be a swallow on this bitterly cold windswept day and still only the 29th of March? But a swallow it most assuredly was. Passing resolutely overhead it plodded on towards Coalport and possibly far beyond. How often have I wondered if that lone swallow ever survived. Such an insignificant event and yet it has always stuck in my memory. After all six thousand miles is a long way to fly!

When we got a good local thunderstorm and the resultant surge of muddy water came down stream the local eel fishermen lost no time in getting cracking They arrived of an evening prepared to fish well into or even through the night. So far as I know they used hooks baited with lobworms unlike their fellow eel fishers on the Wye who fished for them with a clot, or if you prefer a bundle made up of worms and red wool.

Of course the pike also had its devoted band of followers. Live baiting was their method of choice. Instead of a tin of worms they carried a can of water and in it a few small fish, usually roach. Having selected a likely swim it was a question of tackling up. A great cork float and very often a couple of small cork floats further up the line. Then finally an inmate from the can, presumably the one which drew the short straw, was attached to a treble hook and cast out into the selected swim. Tethered as it was to the big float it always reminded me of the sacrificial goat on a tiger shoot. Many a time I stood and watched hoping to see a pike caught but all I ever did see was the big float giving the odd jig and twitch as the captive swam around. It was clearly a pastime calling for great patience and apparently its devotees had that in large measure. Still where more pleasant place to spend an evening with the curlew piping, buzzard mewing, woodcock roading, an occasional steam train leaving acrid smoke, the odd cock pheasant calling and birdsong all around?

Last thing of an evening I used to go and watch Father fishing for salmon. When it came time to finish he invariably said, "Well this is the last cast" and I invariably said," Go on, have another three for luck." So another three for luck it always was and it became a standing joke. On this particular occasion the third cast got hung up on the river bed and he said "So much for your luck!" Anyway the devon minnow shook free and a moment later was fast again but this time there was something pulling on the end. That was the first salmon I ever saw caught.

Before finally packing up he frequently allowed me a few minutes with whatever rod he had been using at the time. This time it was his spinning outfit, greenheart rod and walnut Nottingham reel. Woven nylon had just replaced woven silk but the trace would certainly have been piano wire. Gradually I had acquired the not inconsiderable skill of using a free running centre pin to cast a bait. On this occasion the devon had swung round with the current and I was beginning to lift the rod tip and reel slowly in to fish the cast out. But the reel stopped turning and what I can only describe as a pulsating surge of power was coming back through line and rod. Nothing more dramatic, just that surge of power and realisation dawned that I was into a salmon. Playing the fish was no great problem. There was nothing dramatic, none of the fireworks which can attend these events and in due course Father gaffed a Severn salmon of seventeen pounds. My first salmon and at the ripe old age of eleven!

What a very fortunate young fellow, for that fish had already seen and refused that very same devon minnow. Moreover it was a warm sultry evening with scarce a breath of wind when the smoke from a passing train hung for long enough in the valley and a rumble of thunder seemed imminent. Anything in fact but a fishing evening! But that is the story of salmon fishing for you. How often Salar bucks all the rules. How often he presents the out and out novice with the catch of the day. How wonderful!

So we look back on those years of the Forties, to a time when I spent countless happy hours on the banks of a great lowland river. To have fished those waters, to have watched and listened to the diversity, that sheer wealth of wildlife, which filled both river and valley, to have such a treasure trove of memories of which I have attempted to describe but a few---I count myself fortunate indeed!

You see the Severn which I fished was still in much the same unspoiled, unpolluted state which had ruled from time immemorial; though there were warning signs things were about to change--- and not for the better. But that is another story, one which is recorded with great clarity and an authority born of years of acute observation by my late father Norman Sharpe in his book Apley Hall.

39. The Last Rick

It would surely have been the last straw rick built in our locality. Perhaps I should explain that before the days of combine harvesters corn was harvested with a machine called a binder which cut the standing crop and tied it into easily handled bundles called sheaves. Unlike the combine it did not thresh, that is separate the grain from the straw. This meant the sheaves had to be stored until threshing could take place; and so they were built into ricks which then required thatching to keep rain out. Then along came the Dutch barn which did away with the need for thatching.

On the occasion of which I write however the Dutch barn was full and there was still a field of oats to harvest. Mick the Irishman was to build the rick and my job was to feed the sheaves to him as they dropped from the top of the elevator. They had to land just ahead of Mick as he built course upon course. Each new course jutted a little farther out than its predecessor so the side of the rick sloped gently outwards. Once the walls were judged high enough the process was reversed and the point at which that took place was called the easing.

How the Devil they judged that point has always remained a mystery to me; for a good rick builder could finish pointing up the ridge as the final sheaf came off the elevator. That was a supreme skill. Anyway you finished up with something the shape of a house with walls and pitched roof. Of course the higher you went the better became the view of surrounding countryside and the supreme irony, certainly not lost on Mick, was that we were able to watch combines working on other local farms!

Next came thatching. Tom Hotch was the man chosen for that job. He promptly disappeared into a nearby copse for a day or two and the result of his labours were the thatch pegs needed for the job; eighteen inch lengths of hazel sharpened to a point at one end. Had they been for a hay rick they would only have been twelve inches long, or so he informed me, for I had been the man earmarked to help him.

Next came preparation of the straw; last season's wheat straw which had been threshed and tied in boltens (bundles). Preparation involved selecting lengths of good straw and stripping the flag (leaf) off them by pulling through a great horny hand; then retying into bundles. Then there was the winding of binder twine on to sticks to create bobbins which would reach the length of the rick.

Preliminaries complete Tom ascended the ladder to the roof of the rick and I followed behind with a couple of bundles on a pitchfork. Starting at the bottom edge he carefully cut the band and eased out a layer of straw. Unlike the thatch on a house it was no more than an inch deep and I marvelled that it would turn rain. Once there the thatch was kept in place by pegging the far side, pulling the twine across and pegging the near side. Then up far enough for the next layer to overlap the one below, all the time bemoaning that wheat straw used to grow to a decent length and a man could make a decent job of thatching. Lord alone knows what he would have had to say about your modern short- strawed varieties. It certainly could not have been broadcast before 9.0 pm –if at all!

So there you are. Surprisingly quickly we worked our way from end to end and then along the other side. Sheep shears were used to trim a neat bottom edge to the glistening roof which would indeed shed rain efficiently until threshing day arrived. It was a farming craft which called for immense skill from both builder and thatcher, often the same fellow, and produced those veritable works of art which used to adorn the countryside. I have always been grateful for having had the opportunity to have taken part in the building and thatching of the last corn rick in the district.

40. Rough Justice

Denzil was but a lad of thirteen when it all happened. He met Grandfather who greeted him with, "Hi-up I've been lookin' for you lad. I've got a job wants doin". Doesn't sound too promising thought Denzil but the old man went on: "I'll pay you well too lad.". Sounds better thought Denzil and followed the old boy back to his house. The job, it transpired, was painting the guttering. So up the ladder went Denzil complete with paint pot and brush. Needless to say Grandad supervised from below; every so often Denzil had to move the ladder back and make good a patch he had missed - - easily enough done when painting gutters. So back and forth it was until they finally got round the cottage and painting the down pipe completed the job. Glory be!

Now to get paid thought the worker - but nothing appeared to be happening in that department."You did say you were going to pay me" he finally ventured.

"Ah, so I did lad, and so I will". With that Grandad fished out his purse, one of the old horse shoe variety, which he opened to pull out the contents. A pound note, a ten shilling note, three or four half crowns and a shilling; we are talking pre-decimalisation incidentally.

Looks promising thought Denzil, then watched with increasing concern, even disbelief as first the pound note, then the ten shilling note, then the half crowns disappeared one by one to leave just the shilling - five pence in modern speak! He's never going to offer me that thought Denzil, but offer it he did with the air of a man bestowing a fortune.

"Well" said our worthy, "If you're as hard up as all that per'aps you'd better hang on to it!" With that he made off down the village where he met two or three of his pals and spent a convivial hour or so.

All in good time the worker wended his way home where, with scant ceremony, his old man laid hold of him and proceeded to administer a tidy walloping.

"What was that all about then", bleated Denzil?

"That was for being rude to your grandfather! That's what!"

41. Scything Matters

If there is one thing this heavy old land of ours can grow it is thistles. We can grow thistles of a size and in a profusion which beggars belief. "Cut a thistle in July and it is sure to die", goes the old saying. Like many another old sayings it is stronger on rhyme than reality but cutting does at least steady the wretches for the rest of the year.

During the merry month of May when lambs frisk and thistles rush to join them, I rang our neighbour to make the usual arrangement. Come early July Horace would appear complete with tractor and mower and that would be that. But a fortnight into July I was beginning to experience that certain uneasy feeling. Yes, you can guess it. You see Horace shares the machinery with his brother, a fatal arrangement at the best of times. Harvest being early, the tractor was on trailer duty. Spring barley, then rape, then wheat, the weeks would fly and so too the thistledown. All much appreciated by the local bees, birds and butterflies, but not alas, the neighbours.

Horace having jiggered the job and no one else wanting to know about it, there was nothing for it but to make for the back of the woodshed and reach down the old scythe. Armed with that piece of Iron Age automation one man went to mow. On our way who should we drop across, the scythe and I, but the stonemason who happens to have a workshop round the corner. Ancient his craft may be but the mason is your modern man. Not for him the mallet and chisel. No sir! Having spent the day slicing and shaping lumps of stone with an assortment of diamond tipped blades and power tools, he zips into multicoloured leathers, bestrides his mistress and joins the "Ton Up

Brigade". So far I have resisted all his earnest exhortations to "have a go on the pillion - promise I'll go steady". Steady at what - ninety miles an hour?

On spotting the scythe, ill-concealed pity and condescension fairly radiated from him. "Why the hell don't you get yourself a strimmer instead of farting on with that ruddy old thing?" Somewhat nettled, and not a little embarrassed on the scythe's behalf, I protested here was a tool which had helped shape civilisation itself. Still more to the point what about a bit of respect in the presence of an endangered species? By that of course I meant one of the mugs still able to use said tool. "Anyway," my oration concluded, "You can stuff your damn strimmers. I can't stick the filthy, noisy, stinking little brutes!"* Totally unimpressed the mason went his way and the scythe and I went ours.

Now the beauty of scything lies, not only in the fact you can hear the birds sing, you can also hear yourself think. You can think for example, that on reaching a certain age, there is rather more to look back on than to look forward to. Surely then we can be forgiven if the old mind is allowed to wander away on its own, right away down memory lane, in fact to the time it first began to garner memories. Back to the time a little lad used to shadow a chap called Sidney when that worthy went to scythe the Pithole; a flat area with steep sides where local folk maintained clay had once been dug. Fruit trees flourished there and in a wet season shallow ponds formed in parts of it. Cow parsley, nettles, docks and coarse grasses grew in profusion beneath the trees, creating a paradise for frogs and the grass snakes which hunted them.

Sidney scythed away and I followed close behind complete with bucket and makeshift lid. As he disturbed the frogs I chased and caught them. Into the bucket and on with the lid until it became impossible to get another one in without allowing an inmate to escape. Then Sidney stopped scything and accompanied me to the centre of the mown area where the bucket was ceremoniously upended. A tidal wave of frogs, large frogs and small, olive green and ochre frogs, all the colours of young leaf in Spring went flying and leaping to regain the sanctuary of the unmown herbage. Having enjoyed a good laugh at the spectacle Sidney returned to the scything and I started filling the bucket again.

We still have an old pykel here which I use for feeding hay to the sheep. Really it is worn out and should have been replaced long ago;

but you see it is the one Sidney used around the stable at home. It may seem strange to you, but for me taking hold of it remains a form of contact, a shaking of hands as it were, with the fellow who once used it.

Then there were the roadmen of my schooldays. A shovel, a broom, a barrow, a scythe and two red flags made up their inventory of equipment. Where you saw a strip of verge left unscythed you could guarantee a local gamekeeper had spotted a nesting pheasant or partridge and let the roadman know. Quite amazing how often nesting gamebirds select roadside verges, they really are not the brightest! Wise keepers made mighty certain the roadman did not go short of a rabbit.

There was one lovely old boy who tended the roads around home. He sported a huge beard and was known as Jesus to the less devout. Come knocking off time he carefully tied both broom and shovel to the crossbar of his cycle. Then, very meticulously he tucked his trousers into cycle clips. That seen to, he proceeded to push the bike all the way back to the village. Local rumour maintained he had been known to ride the machine though I never actually found anyone who could vouch to having seen him.

On leaving school and starting work on the farm Tom Hotch took me in hand; something for which I have always been grateful. Tom had left school and arrived at work to find himself stuck in the middle of a scything gang. Beginners were always put there so they had to keep up with the pace. A bit of help sharpening the blade to begin with and then they were on their own. "Believe me", said Tom, "you soon learned how to sharpen her"! At that time a man reckoned to scythe an acre of hay in a day, or two acres of corn. That, you may take it from me, was work!

Tom had grown up in the same parish as the legendary Tom Dutton, a giant of a man with strength to match. I forget now whether it was 7 acres or 9 acres, what's the odd acre or two -but that was the size of the cornfield he once scythed between two sunrises. As you may guess there was serious money riding on the outcome. So too when Tom's father once watched him carry three sacks of wheat the length of a barn, one under each arm, the third across his shoulders. Bearing in mind those sacks weighed 18 stones apiece; we can safely say men was men in them thar days!

Small wonder then that Tom could fairly make the old scythe talk when he and his protégé were sent to "open out" areas around the gateways into cornfields. That was so the horses and binder could get

in and "set up" without trampling the corn. Tom did the scything and my job was to gather the mown corn and tie it into sheaves with bands of straw. Given the chance, when for instance the boss is scything thistles, the old memory loves to dwell on the likes of Tom. Amazing fellow, he was an absolute master of the endless range of skills essential to the farming of those days. Hedge laying, draining, thatching, ploughing, rick building, care of livestock and by the time I knew him, he was a dab hand with a tractor and eventually took over the wheel of a combine. From scythe to combine all in a lifetimes work! Just think of that!

But having wandered away and browsed in the sunny pastures of youth the poor old memory has eventually to work its way back to the present. Long gone are the scythe and its brushing hook cousin as the prime means of trimming and tidying Mother Nature. Nowadays flail mowers and strimmers assault the eardrums as they leave their pulverised trail. Hardly a daisy, let alone a dandelion, dare raise its head on the manicured verges of the village road where once the roadman grazed his goat. Where I wonder would Tom Hotch's rooster and his harem scratch for their living now? And what about Sidney's pig at the bottom of the garden?

Scything the last of the thistles I imagine the look on that worthie's face were he able to have seen the folk vieing to buy up his cottage. "But what the hell", he would ask "do they want my old place for? I mean people like that with money?' Ah but they dream of the peace and quiet and tranquillity of village life I would have explained. Alas their dream is but a mirage for they dream of something which no longer exists. That world vanished years ago when Sidney, Tom Hotch and the roadman made way for the combustion engine.

For now the traffic roars and thunders through the village, lawn mowers rip and rev, hedge trimmers whine and chatter. And strimmers scream! Filthy, stinking, noisy little brutes! That methinks is where we came in, the scythe and me. A marvellous tool is a scythe. Gives time for the memory to wander and browse, and is quiet enough to let a man think. Good exercise too - provided the old back and muscles can still take it!

42. Sixty Years On

Come breakfast time fine weather saw us arrayed along a hedge bank whilst in the sky above larks sang their little hearts out: foul weather found us sitting beneath a Dutch barn where farm pigeons and sparrows serenaded us. On reflection what a mixed bunch we were: horny-handed veterans of a lifetime's toil on the land deigning to mingle with callow youths who, willing though we were, still had a deal to learn - something of which we were often reminded!

And what better place to learn than that hallowed break from work when farm staff sat down together to eat, to gossip and argue, to reminisce, recollect and generally put the world in order. Village gossip, local scandal- usually an abundance of that! National, indeed international events, sport; all competed with rude jokes, last night's radio programmes - would Dick Barton escape yet again- together with the spicier nuggets from yesterday's papers. An infinite range of topics, some ludicrous, others serious, served to generate a happy mixture of ribaldry, profound wisdom, biting sarcasm, the driest of straight faced dry humour; even unrestrained hilarity as occasion demanded.

Mostly forgotten, hardly surprising as I am going back over sixty years, yet fragments remain etched on the old memory as clearly as though it were but yesterday. Come to think of it I often struggle to recall what the devil did happen yesterday!

At that time we were watching the demise of the working horse. Predictably the veterans mounted a stoic defence of their old comrade. But they knew, oh they knew alright, that the future lay with the machine; and boy had they got it all worked out.

"You young blokes- often they called us other things- have got it made You'll have none of the back-break. You'll get twenty quid (pounds) for a thirty five hour week an' four weeks holiday a year." At the time it was six pounds for a forty five hour week and one week's holiday; only to be taken of course when you could be spared. That often fell when the sugar beet campaign ended and spring work had not begun! Their reasoning was logical, indeed profoundly so. Where oh where, I have often pondered since, did it all go so badly wrong?

Of course World War II was but a recent memory. In fact many a farm worker was still wearing out his old uniform. Yet it seemed the world had still not had enough of war. Russia in Europe and China in Asia; all the ingredients for more carnage. But what to do about it - that was the problem. Harold, bless his heart had the perfect solution. "Let them as wants wars fight the buggers!" Though spoken in all serious-ness it was seized upon with alacrity.

Churchill-v-Hitler and Trueman-v-Stalin: three by three minute rounds and may the best man win! It was naturally assumed of course that old Winnie and friend Trueman would be up to the job. Some concern was expressed regarding Winnie's condition, but no worry, a puff or two on the old cigar and a tot of whisky between rounds should see our man through. But who would referee? Why the Pope and Archbishop of Canterbury of course - who else? All this with due solemnity until finally it was all too much for one or other of us lads; and then hilarity reigned supreme.

What chinwag would have been complete without giving politics and politicians an airing --- a little going over as it were? The latter were no problem. They were quickly dispatched, in jocular if somewhat summary fashion, the general consensus being you could not believe a word the buggers said! So what has changed?

But politics? Ah now that was an altogether different kettle of fish. That only fools and horses sweat was undeniable and we harboured no illusions. We were firmly in that category. But what the devil to do about it? Now that was the burning question. Every other workforce in the land seemed to be striking for what they wanted and invariably getting their way. At no time though can I ever recollect striking being seriously discussed as an option. The old hands were well aware they had sweated all their lives for a paltry wage. They also knew they were highly skilled, absolute masters of their craft, and without them farming stopped. Loyalty, lack of organisation amongst other things may all be cited, but I really believe the one thing which maintained the peace was the fact the vast majority enjoyed their work. As though to reassure themselves they often drew comparison with the boring humdrum existence of industrial workers. You guessed it. We never did quite decide how the cake was going to be cut more fairly!

Of course sport was an entirely different matter. There we all had the answers, though on only one was there general agreement; and that was why the Aussies consistently beat us at cricket. Simple! They had not had food rationing during the war! So much for the Aussies then; but what about those Hungarians, the "Magical Magyars" not merely beating, but thrashing us at football. And at Wembley too the cheeky bounders! Now that really was a nasty one and produced some fanciful explanations. The possibility they might just have been better footballers was never even considered. No sir! If nothing else we were British to a man!

Not so though where our local idols, the then mighty Wolverhampton Wanderers were concerned. In those long forgotten halcyon days they won far more often than they lost, but when such tragedies did occur there was no shortage of opinion, expert opinion at that, regarding both tactics and talent-or lack of. Had he but had the great good fortune to listen to us Stan Cullis the Wolves manager could have learned a trick or two.

Then there were local events. Had we lads who strove mightily for the honour of the village at cricket or football had the misfortune to lose at the weekend, then Monday mornings could be an uncomfortable experience. "Never seen such a show. What the bloody 'ell was yer playin' at?" We really suffered badly at the hands of our elders and betters; they who, in their day, had performed equally badly if not worse. General opinion was it would have been better had our mothers never had us- or words to that effect.

Shooting and hunting were part of our world and sparked but little argument. Only Tom spoke up in defence of the fox. "Arr an they wouldner be so keen on chasin' the poor buggers if they'd got machine guns up their arsoles". Bond had yet to be invented but Fleming was never going to beat that one. Tom could never understand why such overwhelming logic only produced hilarity. It was simple enough to him and he became distinctly tetchy. Not half as tetchy though as when local gossip tipped us off that the "long tailed un" had raided his hen run with devastating results. Innocent enquiry as to how his hens were

laying really brought the worst out in him.

Mention of that worthy brings another story to mind. Tom hailed from foreign parts, or to be more exact, the North of the county. The farm he had worked on had a head waggoner whose party piece began with him pushing a muck fork into a muck hill. Then a carthorse was hitched to the fork and given the old gee-up. Pull as it might, and Tom who was no mean raconteur, told how the traces could even be heard creaking under the strain; that horse could not move the fork Can you believe that one? No? Nor did anyone else and we lads ribbed Tom unmercifully. "Ah well, you young buggers know it all of course. But I seen it with me own eyes, and more'n once"

Not long ago I happened across a book about the Suffolk Punch carthorse by George Ewart Evans. Right there on page 109 he related how he had been told of the identical trick being performed by a Suffolk horseman. His description echoed Tom's, even down to the creaking of the traces. Evans had accepted the validity of the account, but unlike other horsy stunts for which he provided convincing explanations, could hazard no guess as to how that one was done.

Was I dreaming, or did I hear a familiar voice in my ear? A voice which spanned sixty years or more. "Now then you young bugger! Howse about that? Didner I tell yer?

43. Fortified Wine

A seasoned warrior for the rights of walkers (The Ramblers), the Major had been a constant thorn in the flesh of many a local landowner and farmer. One farmer in particular had crossed swords with him on many heated occasions. So too had his farm foreman.

Imagine his surprise then when he answered a knock on the door to find the Major standing there. Here we go again thought he, but would you believe it, the Major was in conciliatory mood. It transpired he had noticed the walnut trees in the farm orchard and wondered whether, as a great favour of course, he might be allowed to tap their rising sap in the Spring? He explained wine making was a great hobby of his and walnut wine was his speciality. His technique was the same as used in the tapping of syrup from maples and would not damage the trees

Temptation! Mighty temptation! But what the hell? The fellow's been a total pain in the arse for years but obviously there is a better side to him. A wine maker? Who would have guessed it? Well well! He'll turn out to be a hunt supporter yet. So yes! Help himself to the walnut sap and welcome. But don't let me forget to tell the foreman: bound to be an almighty bust-up if he catches the Major in the orchard.

A month or so later the farmer and his foreman were chatting. Said the farmer, "Oh by the way I saw the Major the other day. Told me the walnut wine had turned out magnificently."

"Bloody should 'ave too," chortled the foreman. "'Cos I pissed in it!"

44. Georgie

We often fished a stretch of the Severn known as The Roving. On the opposite bank there were two dwellings. One which had a small-holding attached to it was occupied by a family and the man of the house worked on a local farm. In the other, a couple of hundred yards down river, dwelt Georgie.

When first I began going to the river with Father he was usually to be seen working his garden or tending his beehives in the orchard beyond. Lord knows how many he had, certainly some scores, even a hundred it was rumoured. At some stage during the evening he invariably walked up the river side to his neighbours and collected a can of milk. Never stayed there long, just a brief chat and then away. On the way back downstream he always stopped again to exchange a few words with Father. Then, as the sand martins and swallows hawked, swifts wheeled and screamed, a nightingale led the woodland chorus and a Severn Valley steamer puffed and rattled its way to Coalport, Georgie returned to his solitary existence.

And believe me – it was solitary! Those dwellings, like several others I can well recall along the banks of the Severn, were quite unbelievably isolated. Their only links with the outside world were either a long footpath leading up through the wooded hillside known as Brown's Covert which climbed away from the river, or a rough cart track which ran for a mile upstream through fields to Coalport.

Even at that time some of those riverside dwellings were beginning to fall into disuse and dereliction. Local lore maintained they had originally been associated with the barge traffic on the river. That surely was the only feasible explanation for their situation. Georgie's abode was certainly getting to look very neglected. It is extremely doubtful whether it had piped water and it certainly had no electricity or telephone. What his background was, or indeed what had led him to choose that outdated and reclusive way of living, no one seemed to know.

But then of course Georgie had not always been as retiring. The head forester of the day at Apley used to tell how one evening he had walked over to buy honey from Georgie. After settling up for the honey he was offered a glass of mead. For those less familiar with the traditions of rural life mead is an alcoholic beverage made from honey --- and it packs a punch! One glass led to another and the pair of them soon got down to the serious business of evaluating the new season's vintage in convivial fashion.

Daylight had long since given way to darkness when the forester finally left to walk home through Brown's Covert. When he eventually awoke next morning the sun was well up in the heavens and, to his astonishment, --- he was still in Brown's Covert! And to quote his very words ---"Was them ruddy bees a-buzzin'!"

My earlier recollections of Georgie involved a donkey. Local hearsay had it that in winter the donkey was fitted up with green glasses to persuade him to eat dead bracken. Well it's a good story! This animal was used to carry honey, and doubtless the odd few bottles of mead up to Coalport. On the return journey it carried provisions and supplies. These would almost certainly have included coal at one time but as the years went by Georgie managed to develop his own source of that commodity. Here is how.

One summer's evening Father had taken a break from fishing and was sitting on the river bank opposite Brown's Covert. Imagine his surprise when a fellow came floating downstream in a coracle. Just before the head of Brown's run he manoeuvred it expertly into the far bank and stepped ashore. It was Georgie. Did his mastery of that little craft offer a clue to his background I wonder? Anyway the Severn was at a dead low summer level and, after a good look around, the navigator rapidly set about removing rocks from the edge of the stream. In no time he had exposed something black and was very soon loading lumps of it into the coracle. Once it was full he took the end of a long rope and pulled the little craft back upstream and out of sight.

Half an hour later Georgie came floating down again for a second

load. After getting this one he carefully replaced the stones to cover the seam. At that point Father made his presence known by hailing him across the river. He immediately regretted doing so for the poor old boy was in a terrible state, fearing his source of winter heating would be a secret no longer. He need not have worried. Without doubt Father never told another soul other than myself.

There must have been several of these seams running out to the surface in that neck of the woods. There was certainly one a mile down the valley in the Apley woods. During the General Strike in the 20's that one had been opened up to supply coal for the Hall.

But back to Georgie. Alas, as the years went by the donkey disappeared and was not replaced. His house became ever more run down and when fishing opposite one no longer caught sight of him tending bees or garden. Lord alone knows what he lived or scraped by on, or indeed how he managed at all, for he could surely have collected little in the way of pension or benefits.

So now to complete the story. One fine summer's day, when just about to sit down to tea, Father realised there was a car in the yard. He went out to see who it was and a fellow was getting out of a chauffeur-driven limousine. He walked across to Father and introduced himself in a broad Australian accent. He said they had stopped in Norton and someone had suggested Father might be able to help find the man they were looking for. It gradually began to dawn on Father that this amiable and obviously very wealthy Aussie was none other than a brother of our friend Georgie. A fairy tale ending to this story then you are beginning to think? Alas no. Sadly poor old Father had to break it to this pleasant man that Georgie had died but a couple of months earlier

It must have been a shattering end to his dream of finding a long lost brother after travelling so far. Anyway on Father's suggestion he went out and brought in his chauffeur and they all sat down to tea together. Then Father led the Aussie along the top of the Spring Coppice to a point where there was a break in the timber and they could stand to gaze out across the valley to where Georgie's old dwelling nestled between Brown's Covert and Severn Stream. From that distance it still looked snug and comfortable, almost idyllic indeed. The poor fellow could take back to Australia a picture of where his brother had lived out his life in a place of tranquillity and great beauty. A place where the martins and swallows hawked, swifts screamed and the nightingale led the woodland chorus.

45. Tom Oliver

L eaving Astol farm and heading towards Stockton the road crosses
a tiny stream. It was there that my father noticed parked cars and
a group of fellows in the adjoining meadow. Curiosity aroused he too
pulled up and walked across to add to the numbers; the estate agent,
farm manager, clerk of the works and a couple of the farm fellows with
spades.

It appeared the gathering was all about locating a land drain.
A thorough search for its outlet into the stream had drawn blank. So
what the Devil to do now? Father suggested they could do worse than
seek the help of Tom Oliver; a master of his craft, he had worked at
Astol many the long year and could well have laid the drain. Good idea
said the agent and immediately went in search of Tom who was long
since retired and living in the village.

They had not long to wait before he got back together with Tom.
That worthy paced one way and then back the other and then stopped.
"The trouble is", said he " you've taken the hedge out which used to run
down here and that's muckin' me up". Tom began pacing again, first
one way,then back, each time shortening the distance. Finally he
banged his heel in the turf. "Try her there then!".

Have you ever dug for a tile drain knowing its approximate whereabouts but not its exact position? You begin by digging a hole and
having drawn blank extend a trench to the left. Finding nothing to the
left you then extend the trench to the right; more to the left; more to
the right until finally—glory be there is a trickle of water and final
triumphant delving reveals the top of a tile drain.

It is a eureka moment because take it from me finding a drain can be a mighty long, arduous and frustrating affair. Those fellows with spades would have known the score only too well and begun digging down from Tom's heel mark with a deal of hope but precious little anticipation. Oh ye of little faith! A couple of spade lengths down and there was the trickle. They had gone straight down onto a pipe laid thirty, forty more likely fifty years before.

Why make so big a deal of locating a blocked field drain. Lets just say it is my small tribute to fellows like Tom Oliver, men of immense skill and sheer physical endurance who, together with their forebears, crafted and maintained the farming and countryside we live in today.

46. Nothing Is For Ever

Ever wondered what it was like when Grandad was a lad? Come to that was Grandad ever a lad? Believe it or not he was and he is going to tell you what life was like in the rural areas of the West Midlands during the 1930s and early 40s. He, or rather I, for I am he, am going to tell you because when my grandparents told me a little of life in their young days I found it mighty interesting.

How for instance as a young teenager Grandpa Davis drove his pony and trap through the Bull Ring to deliver milk into the middle of Birmingham: how Grandpa Sharpe walked many a mile from Hexham into Newcastle or maybe Southshields or Wallsend to watch ship launchings or the topping-out ceremonies on Armstrong's new factory chimneys. How Grandma Davis took over running of farm house and home aged thirteen and Grandma Sharpe watched the Culler Coates lassies hawking herrings around the streets of Newcastle –one a penny in the morning- five a penny come evening!

Unfortunately they told me all too little. So, in writing this for you I hope to avoid that mistake and trust you will find it equally interesting and gain some insight into how we old fogies got to be as we are.

Suppose I begin by taking you into a typical country dwelling of the 1930s? Imagine it's dusk – so you look for the light switch. But you look in vain. Your switch will be a box of matches to light the candle on the mantlepiece or the paraffin lamp on the table. Why no switch? Well the awful truth is – there ain't no electricity! Now stop for a moment. Stop and think of all your present lifestyle props powered by electricity. Forget them. They exist only in rudimentary form in a few more favoured residences supplied by an embryonic grid. Believe me the range of appliances available really was limited: for the most part electric fires, clothes irons, small cooking hobs, and radios. Nor was our knowledge of the new medium any too hot. Not satisfied with its output a pal of mine took the fire poker to their new electric fire. Result- a blinding blue flash, a bird's nest of wire element and our friend on his back somewhat shocked!

Most folk did manage to afford a battery driven radio. Just to confuse the issue the batteries were called accumulators; housed in square glass jars with red and black terminals they needed regular charging so everyone had a pair of them. Friday evenings saw a procession of fellows on bicycles fitted with carbide lamps taking the accumulator for its recharge.

So you fancy a nice warm bath after a hectic day? Forget it—unless of course it happens to be Friday evening when the whole family take their turn to freeze in a zinc bath in front of the kitchen range. Shower, hair driers, what are they? And speaking of hair, that was a once weekly job, usually with soap, soft water from the rain water butt with a spoonful of vinegar in the rinsing water guaranteed to impart a shine. Some swore by beer instead and you can bet it did not all go in the rinse!

If you were lucky there would have been a cold water tap indoors, otherwise it would have been a pump over the well in the yard. A few more affluent properties did have a bathroom with hot and cold but even for them central heating was years away.

For most folk the toilet was still the wee house out the back. For those taken short during the night, or just not fancying a trip out into icy darkness, there was always that marvellous chinaware utensil variously named the chamber pot, the po, the guzunder, or simply the piss pot. This aid to comfort normally resided beneath the bed or, in more refined circumstances, in a wooden chamber cabinet which doubled as bedside table. Getting out of bed and stepping into a half filled potty was an experience best avoided!

Earlier I mentioned the kitchen range. Burnished and black-leaded that cast iron, coal gobbling creation, its open fire sandwiched between a boiler on one side and an oven on the other was at the very heart of daily life. First job in the morning was to get the fire going. That done it heated water, boiled kettles and saucepans, warmed wash-day flat irons, dried wet clothing and boots and – glory be, created warmth.

True, most houses did have an open fire in an adjacent sitting or best room but those old ranges were at the very heart of life. Perhaps it should be added that with coal being rationed and paraffin more readily available many kitchens acquired a three ring oil burner during the war. A portable baking oven could be placed over two of the rings.

Life on the domestic front was rigorous to say the very least. Kitchens, sculleries, pantries, invariably had brick or tile floors which had to be scrubbed. In farmhouses dairies and long passages had to be added to the list. Scrubbing was a hands and knees job using lumps of coarse soap cut from a long block. Oak floors were polished whilst pine or deal were either stained and polished or covered with linoleum which again was polished-again a hands and knees job. Mansion polish, that was the great standby. It must have been manufactured by the score indeed hundred of tons. Fitted carpets were unheard of and their lesser brethren got their come-uppance with arm-driven carpet sweepers. Brooms, dusters, feather dusters, mops, dustpans and brushes completed the housewife's armoury.

Now to dwell on that annual ritual of domesticity - Spring cleaning. As was appropriate for the bed-rock, the very core of good house-keeping it created massive upheaval. Carpets were taken outside to be hung over the linen line and beaten until they squealed or at least until dust ceased to fly. Believe me that could take some time for the amount of dust held by a carpet was nye unbelievable. Furniture was heaved away from walls to reveal dusty cobwebs and bolting black beetles which duly caught it hot. Curtains unhung for washing, pictures unhung, altogether an unsettling time for the resident spiders; drawers and wardrobes to empty and last year's lavender bags to be replaced with new. Some households used mothballs, camphor I think, anyway it was not hard to tell when you met the owners! Cupboards were emptied, so too pantry shelves and the ladies of the house indulged in a fearsome dusting, scrubbing, china washing, beating and polishing frenzy. It was not the time, I promise you, to go in with dirty boots! But why all the fuss? Put simply it was the base line for the cleanliness which at that time was the one and only weapon against the likes of clothes moths, bed bugs, lice, nits, fleas which once installed were proof against all the wondrous remedies around at the time, even the fail-me-never cures passed down by the grannies

When you consider the amount of hard graft involved in running a 30's home it is amazing the womenfolk managed to go out to work.

But many did; seasonal jobs on the land, potato picking, weeding, beet hoeing, stone picking, to name but some. Others did part time work in larger more affluent residences. Busy ladies!

Power on the land was supplied mainly by muscle; muscle from man and muscle from the horse. My generation saw the final demise of the working horse during the 40s and early 50s They were replaced by the tractor, very slowly at first during the 30s and then at an ever increasing pace throughout the 40s. Possibly the horse was glad to be rid of the toil though I always felt that, apart from killing work like timber hauling, they really enjoyed life.For the men who had worked them it really was a sad time. No longer were they the very kingpins of the work force and I do know some of them felt it keenly.

Human muscle too was just beginning to be replaced by machinery – and a damn good thing too! Who would wish to go back to hand pulling sugar beet or spreading muck with a hand fork? Who would want to hump 16 stone, that is 224 pounds, or for the uneducated, 100 kilo bags of corn up granary steps without a handrail? Or would you fancy trudging home, boots and clothing soaked through, and mud and muck up to your knees day after day? Hours worked were far too long and the work itself far too hard.

Perhaps then, a moment for me to give way to temptation and for you to turn a deaf ear. A suitable moment none the less to reflect that but for the graft, sweat and physical hardship of earlier generations we should not be living the life of Riley we all take for granted today.

Also too, an opportune moment to dwell on a little story recounted but recently by a Norfolk landowner. Walking his property one day he came upon an old employee, long since retired, but who still came to do a bit of work on the place. "Henry" said he, "You've seen some changes on the land in your time. What would you say has been the greatest advance of them all"? "Well boss" came the reply, "That's easily answered. It would have to be the gumboot". I think that says it all!

Few houses had a telephone. Ours was one which did. For most folk a single telephone kiosk in the village was the sole means of outside communication. Take correct coinage, convince the operator the number required was Wellington Salop and not Wellington Somerset and you would be connected. I still retain the callout arrangements for the local Home Guard platoon commanded by my father. He had just 6 numbers with which to call out nearly 40 men. The plan was simple. Ring each lucky phone owner who then dashed to alert others in his immediate vicinity. "Wake up mate—We're being invaded!" Doubtless the Nazi hordes would have exercised a degree of sportsmanship and waited whilst the home team mobilised.

How often now we hear the term "Cottage Garden", a description usually bestowed upon a mighty expensive floriforous idyll. What utter tosh! I grew up amongst real cottage gardens which had no lawns and were given almost entirely to vegetable growing. It is true most sported a nice little show of flowers, usually alongside a pathway or tucked in odd corners where they were tended by the good lady who brooked no interference. Now those were the real thing. Not only did they look good - they tasted good!

Most cottage gardens had a pigsty at the end of them. Its occupant resided in some luxury and cheerfully collaborated in the scratching of ears and back whilst discussion centred "on how the inmate was coming on". It was a ritual clearly enjoyed by both owner and pig. But all good things have to end, and January or February were the pig killing months. Saturday mornings were invariably enlivened by the sound of a pig squealing its last. At 14-18 score of pounds it needed four strong men, the local pig killer complete with sticking knife, together with a small troop of lads hoping to get the pig's bladder to blow up and use as a football.

Sounds cruel? Perhaps so, but what alternative was there? I know all involved would have been only too pleased not to kill the poor old pig, for it was all too easy to become fond of them. But it was a question of laying by twelve months supply of good food. And the great thing was, not a single scrap, not one solitary morsel was going to be wasted. That "the only unusable bit was the squeal" was more than just a saying – it was a fact. What about the tail you ask? Well you have got me there but I will guarantee you lot have eaten your share of pigs' tails in all those awful burgers you scoff.

Many properties also kept a small flock of laying hens in a wire netted run, usually like the pig at the end of the garden They were home to traditional breeds, Rhode Island Reds, Light Sussex, White Sussex, Wyandots, Plymouth Rocks or Red, Black or White Leghorns. Spring and summer brought an abundance of eggs. Winter was a lean time so summer surplus was "put down"; that is preserved in water glass for winter cooking use. Incidentally most hen runs also boasted a cockerel. Clearly there was an inherent belief that, apart from being an adornment, things worked better with a man around the place. As a result the whelkin of Thirties dawns rang to a glorious chorus of roosters.

We dwelt at a time when there was no NHS. Poorer people either joined Health Clubs, Friendly Societies or Insurance Schemes and just hoped the devil they would somehow manage to pay the doctor if it came to that. We did have District nurses who must have been funded by some public body. Worthy souls, they conducted nit hunts in schools, brought babes into the world, saw the dying out of it, extracted beads from kids' ears and beans from up their noses, and when they summoned the doctor he, for "shes" were a rarity in those days, lost no time in attending – at a price of course. In fairness it has to be stressed, most really were family doctors, and indeed waived their charges where there was hardship or poverty. Gratitude was the initial reaction, but how often it became tempered by resentment, for in truth few of us like being "beholden".

There were of course all the usual childhood maladies: two much feared being scarlet fever and diphtheria which both appear to have gone off the radar these days. Common afflictions seldom encountered now were boils, sties, chilblains and heat lumps. My grandmother's sure-fire cure-all for the latter was a nauseous concoction of sulphur and treacle –and Mother, bless her heart, was daft enough to listen to her. TB, that is tuberculosis, was all too common and despite the best efforts of the many TB sanatoria usually proved fatal.

Perhaps I should explain that, apart from cooling, all the milk we drank came straight from the cow. Cattle are carriers of the disease and today herds are tested to eliminate the culprits. In the 30s there was no such practice and it is a certain fact we would all have drunk contaminated milk. Today there is also pasteurisation, another safeguard, but back then the only weapons were cooling and cleanliness. Most people collected their milk in cans directly from the farm or it was delivered by fellows with a pony and trap. Grandma Davis at the Home Farm had a nose like a truffle hound and woe betide anyone who brought a tainted can. Those cans were the bane of my young life. Walk and push the bike was the order of the day and I can still see that pool of white spreading over a muddy road when I was tempted to ride instead of walk!

Without fridges keeping untreated milk was a work of art. In warm and particularly during thundery weather it turned sour at the drop of a hat. All sounds a bit hazardous, and too often alas it was, but there were compensations. The flavour of full-cream milk straight from the cooler was a pleasure denied nowadays.

Polio, also known as sleeping sickness, appeared in intermittent outbreaks and was feared. Few adults passed middle age without having many or indeed all their natural teeth replaced by the artificial variety or indeed doing without either. Dental surgery itself was a crude and painful process. Antibiotics, indeed most of the mainstream modern drugs were still a thing of the future.

Foreign travel was of course the prerogative of the rich. Apart from going to sea the only real opportunity for the less well off was to join the forces. A journey by express train to a distant city was a major adventure; and of course it was all done with steam locos, dirty filthy beasts – but magnificent none the less. Any one of our children, possibly even our grandchildren will have chalked up as much foreign travel as Granny and me put together.

Whilst on the subject of travel, what about every day transport? Looking back I can only recall 13 car owners in our parish. May be a couple I have missed but that really was it. I can only think of 2 motorcycles and a lady who cut a dash on an autocycle; a sort of cross between a bike and a motorbike. She incidentally had won every gymkhana for miles around in her youth so a change of saddle was a natural progression. Bikes, Shanks Pony or pony and traps were the order of the day. Grandpa Davis drove his beloved pony and trap into Bridgnorth market right into the late 40s. He was the cause of considerable frustration amongst car drivers until he packed up and then he was constantly badgered by worthy folk saying how much they missed seeing the nag. There's a lesson there for you!

Cars were mighty different beasts from the engineering marvels of today. Invariably they had only one windscreen wiper and certainly no heaters or radios. Starting on a cold morning could be some performance. If garaged the bonnet would have been blanketed and if left outside the radiator would have been drained for antifreeze did not exist. Getting the engine to start involved a delicate combination of warm water, choke, self starter and cranking or starting handle. The family always maintained that cranking his beloved Flying Standard caused the demise of dear old Grandpa Davis!

By the time cars had clocked up 30,000 miles there was serious talk of re-bores or decoking. What caused even greater foreboding was engine knocking, a sure sign the big end was giving notice that it would soon be appearing through the side of the crank case.

Youngsters either walked or cycled to school including the local grammar school which in my case was 7 miles away. True there was a village shop, a very good one as it happened, and there were tradesmen, bakers, butchers, fishmongers, with vans; none the less local ladies still needed to get to Bridgnorth on a Saturday. There was no bus or carrier so some walked up to 2 miles to Linley station to catch the Severn Valley Flyer. On return the better organised, or were they the more dominant, were met by husbands or sons on cycles who relieved them of their loads.

By my time the village rozzers had given up carrying an ash plant. Nor did they need to. Invariably large men, often wearing World War I medal ribbons, they were still apt to administer summary justice and reigned supreme over their patches. From your modern crime statistics standpoint they were a dead loss. Of course they were because they prevented crime before it occurred; but boy, did they instil a lasting respect for the law, indeed society in general, in the young And as intelligence gatherers they simply had no equal.

Measured in material terms working people were poor, very poor, by today's standards. Invariably they ate well, but to do so spent half a week's wages. After that the kitchen range had to be fuelled and then there was clothing. Most folk managed quite nicely but there was little to spare for the luxuries which can so easily become regarded as essentials. For the great majority the only pension was the old age variety. A few paid small weekly amounts into insurance schemes- the man from the Pru -but most relied on what they could put aside for old age.

There were a limited number of modest dwellings set aside for pensioners but for many it was a question of living with the family. Consider also that workhouses were still very much in use, and tramps a common sight on the roads.

Clothing was an altogether different kettle of fish from that in use today. For one thing there was no central heating and the clothes we wore reflected the fact. Standard apparel for farm workers was corduroy trousers, the real thing which could almost stand up unaided, a dark grey jacket and waistcoat together with a white shirt studded but collarless. Leather boots and leggings completed the ensemble For their bosses it was much of the same except for riding breeches, hacking jackets and studded collar and tie. Caps and trilbys appeared to please all.

For us lads the choice for trousers was grey flannel, or grey flannel, all worsted of course. Until we entered our teens we wore short trousers whilst the girls wore skirts or gymslips down to their knees and ankle or knee length socks according to season. Navy blue gabardine raincoats were standard issue for all. As for fleeces, anoraks, cagoules, T-shirts, trainers, jeans – what were they?

I have no intention of getting involved in ladies apparel except to say slacks were considered distinctly risqué, whilst painted nails and mock leopard skin coats were indicative of a certain type of lady even though animal fur generally was at the height of fashion. Musquash or mink coats were very much the prerogative of the rich.

So how you probably ask did you poor old souls amuse yourselves? Or perhaps what you really mean is how were we kept amused? No tele, no computer, life must have been Hell! There is an old saying, irritating to be sure, true all the same, that what you don't know about you don't miss. It is equally true we had much which has since disappeared. For one thing youngsters could get together to play a deal more than today. For another there were more places to play.

There was cricket and football and for the more sedate the bowling green. Church choirs and bell ringing were outlets for men whilst the ladies had Mother's Union and the WI. Village pubs were thriving, often hilarious and raucous affairs. Throw in dances, whist drives, sports days, village fetes and flower shows, not forgetting annual visits of fairs and circuses to local towns. Cinemas were beginning to make their presence felt and were usually rated either respectable or a flea pit. And to cap it all there was always the good old steam radio—so long as the accumulator held out.

Two aspects I have not touched upon are the weekly wash day and life in the village school. That is because I have dealt at length with both of them under their own individual headings and am too idle to repeat the exercise here. Anno Domini you understand?

But religion I must mention for it played a significant role in rural life. In the schools which were mainly C of E, which is short for Church of England, religious education played a big part in the curriculum. It should be a matter of some pride to you that your grandfather won the coveted first prize of a prayer book. And probably explains why he can still sing the words of every well known hymn in tune. There were few village churches without their own parson and they all had a choir—ours had 6/8 men and a dozen choir boys. Congregations were large and on high days such as Easter, Armistice Sunday, Harvest Festival they were packed. Christmas Day saw two services, the first 6 am. And the second 7 am. We always attended the later one, the excuse offered that we had Grandma with us and in the Thirties grannies were expected to act their age. Even today I can recall the look of supreme smug satisfaction, their absolute certainty of a place with the saints, on the faces of the departing six o'clockers!

So there you are. A happy and uplifting note on which to say goodbye to the rural world of the Thirties..

47. Times Change

After leaving school, aged fourteen for a guess, Charlie Wall began work with the Winscote beat keeper. That would have been 1870 -1880 or thereabouts. Anyway Charlie was sent off with a bag of corn to feed pheasants. His route lay across a grass meadow and in the meadow was a bull; a very nasty bull as it turned out. Charlie was chased out of the field in a hurry, and duly reported back, not having fed the pheasants.

"Well you come with me lad", said the old boy picking up his 12 bore. Nothing unusual in that as keepers so often carried a shotgun. They duly reached the gate and sure enough an extremely angry bull came grumbling across to challenge them. Charlie made ready to run for it; for no way was that gate going to stop him. His fears proved groundless because, with no further ado, the old boy up with his gun and shot the brute dead.

"Now then lad, you carry on and feed your birds and I'll just pop and tell Mr. who ever the farm tenant was in those days, that I've shot his bull!!"